**Evaluating Educational
Investment**

Evaluating Educational Investment

J. Ronnie Davis
University of Florida

John F. Morrall III
University of Florida
and U.S. Department of
Housing and Urban
Development

Lexington Books
D.C. Heath and Company
Lexington, Massachusetts
Toronto   London

Table 3-1, p. 40, Table 3-2, p. 42, and Table 3-3, p. 43 from *Education and Poverty* by Thomas I. Ribich have been reprinted by permission of the Brookings Institution. Copyright © 1968 by the Brookings Institution, Washington, D.C.

Library of Congress Cataloging in Publication Data

Davis, J   Ronnie.
    Evaluating educational investment.

    1. Education—Economic aspects—United States.
2. Manpower policy—United States. I. Morrall, John F., joint author. II. Title.
LC66.D38   338.4'3   73-11681
ISBN 0-669-90522-4

Copyright © 1974 by D.C. Heath and Company

Published simultaneously in Canada.

Printed in the United States of America.

International Standard Book Number: 0-669-90522-4

Library of Congress Catalog Card Number: 73-11681

To
Irving Jay Goffman

Contents

List of Figures

List of Tables

1

The Concept of Investment in Education

Introduction to Human Capital

Fritz Machlup recently pointed out that educational efforts may be regarded as either consumption, investment, waste, or drag.[1] Education is consumption to the extent that it gives present satisfaction to the student or to others, investment to the extent that it promotes either future nonpecuniary satisfaction or future gains in productivity, waste to the extent that it creates neither pleasure nor productivity either now or in the future, and a drag (or at least a hindrance) to the extent that it renders incompatible individuals' preferences and their employment opportunities. Although we shall touch upon all of these aspects in this study of education, we will place emphasis upon the investment characteristic.

Investment is *anything* that accumulates capital; capital is a stock of assets that yields a stream of income or utility over time; thus income is the product of capital. Despite its apparent simplicity, most economists, until recently, would have objected to this broad usage of the terms capital and income. Due mainly to the efforts of T. W. Schultz and Gary Becker, however, the broader concept of capital has taken a firm position in the mainstream of economic thought.[2] The reason for the revival of interest in the concept of human investment was that investment in plants and equipment could not explain by itself the rapid growth of the presently industrialized countries. When human-capital disparities were added to physical-capital disparities, on the other hand, most of the differences in per capita incomes between countries could be explained. Looking at the differences in per capita endowments of human capital alone, Anne Krueger, for example, has demonstrated on conservative assumptions that over *half* of the differences in per capita income between the United States and the less developed countries can be explained by the differences in human-capital endowments.[3]

The concept of human capital also has caused major reformula-

1

tions of theories in such diverse areas of economics as international trade, the distribution of income, developmental economics, human migration, the economics of family planning, health economics, on-the-job training, and the economics of education. The length of the list is evidence enough that the rebirth of the concept of human capital was among the major theoretical developments in economics in the 1960s.

Similarities with Physical Capital Investment

An investment in education, in health, or even in moving to a new area is each just as much an investment as a new factory or public bridge. An initial expenditure presumably is undertaken in each case with the hope of generating a higher return of net income in the future. For education, the private costs are the direct tuition and fees associated with schooling, the indirect opportunity costs of not being able to work full time, and the loss of leisure. The higher return is the increase in earnings over what that student otherwise would have earned had he not received the extra education. Implicit in applying investment theory to the individual as well as to the businessman is the assumption that both are attempting to maximize their future incomes (including psychic income) in their investment decisions. Thus they undertake the investment which yields them the highest return, given their available information, and they undertake investments (the best first) until the return on investments equals the interest costs of borrowing or the implicit interest cost of using one's own savings.

In addition to being to private individuals a signal indicating where the most profitable investment opportunities lie, persistent differences in rates of return between various types of investment are usually signals to society that market imperfections are resulting in a misallocation of resources. The appropriate public policy response to a higher than average return to primary school should be to invest more resources in primary school education. This rate of return approach, which will be discussed below in some detail, is a fundamental analytical tool of the economics of educational investment.

Another less used procedure to determine the worthiness of an investment is to compare present values of the future stream of earnings and of the educational costs. In fact, if the estimated future earnings of individuals that are due to educational investment are capitalized, a dollar value of the educational capital stock can be estimated. The value of the capital stock of education and on-the-job training has been estimated at $1.2 trillion while the corresponding estimate of the United States physical capital stock was $1.27 trillion.[4] If the other forms of human capital are added to the estimates of educational capital, it is apparent that human capital is actually more important to the United States than physical capital.

If one is to use the theoretical structure that has been developed to explain physical capital investment to try to explain human or educational capital investment, one should delineate carefully the differences and similarities between the two building blocks of development and growth. The differences between investment in human capital and investment in physical capital are mostly in degree, not in kind. Thus one theoretical structure is useful in understanding all types of investment behavior.

Dissimilarities: Differences in Degree

The differences in degree are fairly straightforward. First, the concept of opportunity costs is much more important in human-capital investment than it is in physical capital investment. The major "cost" of education is the foregone earnings of the student, not the tuition and fees. It is true that there are opportunity costs of modernizing a plant in terms of the foregone output while the plant is closed, but these costs are not measured in years of foregone earnings as they are in education and, to a lesser extent, in on-the-job training. The importance of this point is that it is harder to estimate opportunity costs than direct costs. Consequently, the student, as well as the economist, has more difficulty in determining the correct investment decision.

Second, the risks involved in making human-capital investments are much higher than in physical capital, because human capital is more fragile, and the payoff period is frequently of longer duration. When a machine stops working, it always can be repaired by replacing all of its parts, but we have not reached that point yet with man. The payoff period for human-capital investment, particularly educational investment, is of longer duration because not only is the period longer when the investment is actually being made (this is related to the point made above on the importance of opportunity costs), but also the period is longer during which the returns are expected to be higher (about forty-five years in the case of a college education). Both of these characteristics of human-capital investment increase the risk of such an investment and therefore increase the difficulty for an investor to make an economically "efficient" decision. Because of the high risks and the tendency for investors to be risk averters, there is apt to be an underinvestment in human capital relative to physical capital, and there is likely to be misallocation of investment among alternative types of human-capital investment.

Third, many human-capital investments are irreversible, whereas most physical-capital investments can be "undone".[a] If the wrong computer is installed in a plant, it can be replaced, but once one moves one's family from the South to the ghetto, it is expensive to go back. By the same token, once a Ph.D. is earned in aerospace engineering, it is almost too late to earn an M.D. There is not the continual feedback of information to the investor in human capital that there is to the investor in physical capital. The decisions that the human-capital investor must make are more unique to each individual, and more likely to be irreversible. These factors further complicate the decision-making process of the investor, and make our theoretical model less accurate in explaining human-capital investment.

Finally, the business investor is likely to have more information available on which to make his decision than the human-capital investor. This point is really a generalization of the above points as they are all related to the information differences of the two types of investment. Risk, time, uniqueness, and irreversibility elements all serve to make higher, or even prohibitive, the cost of obtaining information for the human-capital case. In addition to the effect of these factors, the costs of different types of training and the differential earnings related to various types of educational investments in forms of migration are probably not as well known to potential human-capital investors as similar information is to businessmen. It should be pointed out that gathering the information is a form of investment itself,[5] and due to the above enumerated characteristics

---

[a]Exceptions here might be investments that change the ecology of an area and cause permanent damage.

of human capital, this information is less likely to be provided in optimum quantities for human investment than for physical-capital investment.

If information is a public good in the sense that the government can provide the same information to more than one individual at practically zero marginal cost, a case can be made for governmental provision to the public at large of information on job opportunities, educational opportunities and opportunities to increase one's earnings through migration. The fact that the human-capital market does not function as efficiently as the physical-capital market does not mean that the theoretical model that treats human capital like any other investment is inappropriate. It does mean that the model should be used with caution when describing human behavior. The model still remains the correct tool for the economist to use in judging whether human-capital investment is optimal or not. It is the economist's role to recognize the shortcomings of the individual's decision-making process and fill in the voids, especially with regard to the lack of information.

Inasmuch as the model represents some sort of standard against which to compare actual behavior, the economist can point out where deviations between actual behavior and ideal behavior occur with a view toward correcting the misallocation of resources. In other words, even if the human-capital investment model does not describe the workings of these markets perfectly, it still can be used as a device to determine whether or not there is too much or too little investment in such areas as primary schools, high schools, junior colleges, hospitals, and so forth.

Dissimilarities: Differences in Kind

The differences in kind between human-capital investment and physical-capital investment have to do mainly with the legal and institutional restrictions that have been placed on human capital. Human capital no longer can be sold or mortgaged: a bank that makes an educational loan cannot foreclose on the loan and sell the property. The effect of these restrictions is, of course, to decrease the amount of investment in human capital relative to tangible capital.

Man is, of course, inseparable from his human capital, and his changeable wants and dislikes, as well as those of others, will affect his opportunities and willingness to work. The phenomenon of discrimination is not important in hiring machines. Discrimination limits human capital investment for those who are discriminated against, both directly and indirectly. Directly, discrimination can prevent entry to a given school, and, indirectly, it can limit one's employment opportunities once schooling has been completed, especially for those groups discriminated against who rationally do not undertake as much human capital investment as they might if they were given more auspicious circumstances. Blacks, for example, drop out of school before whites because further schooling no longer may be a profitable investment if market discrimination limits the increase in expected earnings of further schooling. Finis Welch has found, in fact, that market discrimination that limits the acquisition of schooling for nonwhites is much more important in explaining the black-white income differential than the inferior quality of schooling received by nonwhites.[6] Discrimination, in short, is a factor causing a misallocation of human investment.

Another difference between man and machine not often mentioned is that there is usually some disutility associated with working or schooling for man,[b] while for physical capital there is apt to be disutility associated with idleness. This difference means that aside from income effects, there is a greater cost to idle machines than to idle men. Rates of return that compare the desirability of investment in human, as opposed to physical, capital are biased in favor of human investment for this reason. Economists have treated a $100,000 investment in bonds and a $100,000 investment in education, both yielding a return of $15,000 a year with equal risks as being equally desirable investments. Yet the investment in bonds clearly yields a person the additional return from leisure and the freedom of being "one's own man." This factor should be considered when comparing rates of return from education and physical-capital investments. However, this effect is neutralized to the extent that people do enjoy their work and schooling.

There are a few other major differences between physical-capital and human-capital investment that should be mentioned, which are also related to the different legal and institutional environments in which the two types of capital are found. The institution of marriage

---

[b]There is disutility in the sense that if one was financially secure for life, he would probably not choose the particular occupation that he is in.

and the family usually confines one of the partners, most often the wife, to the immediate labor market chosen by the dominant partner.[7] This phenomenon is less important in larger metropolitan areas and where the wife is less specialized. It is perhaps most acute for husband and wife Ph.D.'s in single university communities. The effect is to cause an underinvestment in education on the part of women and a lower national output.

Tax laws also discriminate against investment in human capital. The direct costs of education are usually not deductible, and when human capital wears out, or becomes obsolete, as it certainly does, it cannot be depreciated and deducted from income as can physical capital. There are also, of course, labor laws establishing maximum work hours for certain types of labor and minimum wages. These do not apply to machines and therefore tend to make investment in machines more profitable than investment in man. Labor unions also restrict the opportunities for work of man, usually more than physical capital. Machines do not belong to unions and do not go out on strike. Thus most of the laws and institutions that have grown up to protect the worker also, at the same time, bias investment in favor of physical capital.

Again, these differences, if they are recognized, can be handled by the economist who is trying to determine which areas of investment need emphasis. Most of them work in the direction of causing an underinvestment in education when the private individual is making the investment decision. Therefore, for the above reasons, estimated rates of return to education can be thought of as being biased downwards in comparison with returns to physical capital.

2

Educational Investment and Resource Allocation

Private and External Benefits

The identification and measurement of the benefits of education are fraught with many difficulties because some of the benefits to an educated person are economic in nature while some of them are noneconomic, and because many of the benefits do not accrue to the person educated or even to his family, but are conferred on altogether other people.[1] The *private* benefits of education are those which accrue to the child or to his parents (or guardians); and the *external* benefits are those which "spill over" to families other than those of the educated, even where it is infeasible to identify the families benefited or the money value of the benefits.[a] The latter effects, variously called "externalities," "spillovers," "neighborhood effects," and "third-party effects," are relevant from a social point of view to any decisions on educational spending. To the extent that they are disregarded, provision of education will be inefficient and inequitable, a point which will be demonstrated below.

Private Benefits

The first task in calculating the benefit side is to estimate the differential lifetime earnings stream by comparing the actual earnings of cohorts standardized except for their differing educational attainments. In Figure 2-1, this is the estimation of area *FEHG*. In practice, this is usually done by looking at the difference in earnings for one year and then extrapolating the differences over the rest of the years. In other words, looking at Figure 2-1, area *FEHG* is estimated from the points *J* and *K* and from knowledge about the average life-cycle path of earnings. The danger with this procedure

---

[a]Two comments are in order. First, since children legally are not responsible members of society, education primarily is a task of adult society. Second, the benefits may be either positive or negative.

is that it implicitly assumes that past earnings differentials will be maintained in the future. A priori, economists would expect that if the demand for a given educational level of manpower were relatively stable over time, then an increase in the supply of this manpower would drive down the actual rate of return to this educational investment. So, if an educational investment was pushed because the rate of return calculated from past data was found to be high, it is likely that, due to the long lag in the educational process, the final rate of return would be lower. In some cases, of course, policymakers may overshoot the mark. This result might be one explanation for the current glut of Ph.D's on the market. Evidence that will be presented later, however, indicates that there has been no secular decline in the rate of return in the United States to primary and secondary education.

One should still use the cross-section data with caution because there have been recent indications of narrowing of earnings differentials between groupings of different educational levels.[2] These assumptions about the future demand for education are implicitly built into the use of rate of return estimated by policymakers. These assumptions should be made explicit and attention must be paid to the future demand for education if rates of return analyses are to be used for allocative decisions by policymakers.[3]

Another problem that arises in using the differential in earnings to calculate the benefits of educational investment is that labor market imperfections may distort the calculated rates of return so that the social rate of return deviates from the private rate of return. For example, if the "sheepskin effect" is as important as some have alleged, namely, that employers pay workers with diplomas more than the value of their marginal product, the private rate of return will be higher than the social rate of return and there will be an overinvestment in this type of education from a societal viewpoint.[4] Most economists, however, reject this view.[5] Rate-of-return analysis actually points out to the economists where the distortions lie, because, with all markets perfectly competitive, all rates of return would be equal. The extremely high rates of return to physicians, first pointed out by Friedman and Kuznets, is evidence that the American Medical Association perhaps has engaged in restrictive practices by limiting the supply of physicians.[6]

A problem much more significant than the first two above is that of identifying groups of individuals identical in all traits except their

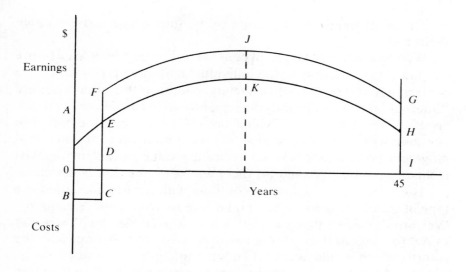

Figure 2-1. Differential Lifetime Earnings Stream

education. Ideally, in order to measure the true effect of education on earnings, all the other factors affecting earnings must be held constant. This is difficult to do because of the high degree of multicollinearity between education and the other factors that influence earnings. Some of these other factors are ability, financial wealth, parents' education, ambition or perseverance, and other types of human capital. This list is not exhaustive. Most studies try to correct for this effect, which, of course, biases rates of return in favor of educational investment. Children with these traits tend to get a higher than average education, yet they would probably have had higher than average lifetime earnings even if they had not had more than average schooling. The procedure used to correct for ability is to use I.Q. tests and standardize the students accordingly. If the sample is large enough, and the demographic data rich enough, researchers can also correct for parents' income, education, social class, the students' race, place of birth, health, and so forth. Many economists still doubt, however, that it is possible to account for all the intangibles such as perseverance, motivation, and personality that may be correlated with both propensity to attain education and propensity to generate higher incomes than normal. This possible bias also must be kept in mind. In addition to the direct monetary effect on earnings, a number of other effects of varying indirectness have been claimed for education by various economists, notably Weisbrod.

Weisbrod lists four types of benefits (other than increased future earnings) which accrue to the individual and three types which are conferred to the remainder of society.[7] Some of the latter types are "internal" to the family and consequently are treated here as private benefits. Those for the individual are (1) the value of the option to continue with further education, (2) the option value of wider employment possibilities, (3) the insurance value of hedging against technological change, and (4) the value of nonmarket benefits.

The value of the option to continue with further education is a type of benefit which one must take care to avoid double-counting. Weisbrod's point is that a seventh grader who is "deciding" whether or not to study at the eighth grade level must consider not only the returns which would accrue if he were to complete it successfully, but also the value to him of the opportunity to proceed to the ninth grade. If he eventually exercises the option to proceed to the ninth grade, however, the value he assigned to the option must be included in the *costs* of the ninth grade. To do otherwise would be to count twice some of the benefits of the ninth grade. Weisbrod has made no attempt to measure the value of this option, perhaps because of the tendency for it to be "washed out" or counted already in earnings studies. (He did make some illustrations of the point, using data from Schultz's studies.)[8]

The second benefit Weisbrod listed was the option value of wider employment possibilities. Here, he seems to have in mind the idea that increased education broadens the range of jobs for which the individual is suited. Although he asserts that a person would attach a positive value to having additional job possibilities, Weisbrod does not measure such values, perhaps because empirically it would be infeasible to distinguish the value of such options and, moreover, because it is not self-evident that his option is "investment." Only to the extent that it reduced uncertainty about anticipated earnings should it be counted in investment calculation. If it only gives a person "satisfaction" to know that other jobs are open to him, then these "phychic" benefits more appropriately would be regarded as consumption.

A closely related benefit which Weisbrod suggests is the insurance value of the hedge against technological change. Whereas the employment option refers to the range of occupations available to a person, the insurance option refers to risks borne in regard to the change of reduced earnings owing to technological changes which give rise to adverse economic effects on his existing occupation. This risk would be reduced if education succeeds in making workers more adaptable to new skills. Again, Weisbrod offers no measurement of this type of benefit. The insurance value also has a consumption element, and only to the extent that it reduces uncertainty about the need to change jobs should such benefits be included in an investment calculation.

Finally, Weisbrod refers to benefits that are nonmarket in nature. He mentions one illustration—the example of literate individuals completing their own income tax returns, arriving at an annual market value of tax return services performed by taxpayers for themselves to be $250 million or a return of about 3.2 percent. There are many problems with this measurement, which, among others, O'Donoghue has cited.[9] Actually, this is a distributional matter. The gains to taxpayers are offset in part by losses to tax accountants, thereby cancelling out part of the effect for the economy as a whole, having little, if any, effect on overall output, and succeeding mainly in redistributing income from accountants to the "rest of the world."

Weisbrod also discusses three types of benefits to persons other than the educated: (1) residence-related benefits, (2) employment-related benefits, and (3) benefits to society in general. Some of the residence-related benefits are "internal" to the family, and consequently, are private benefits which should be numbered among those already discussed. Two such types of benefits are (1) child-care services to mothers, and (2) benefits which may accrue to any future children of the educated.

For the mother (or father) of a school-age child, a valuable child-care service is provided which makes it possible for the mother (or father) either to seek employment or to engage in leisure or other nonwork activities. The effect is in the form of consumption benefits to the extent that mothers (or fathers) choose leisure or simply enjoy reduced anxiety. An economic value is attached to seeking employment. Weisbrod estimated these economic benefits to be approximately $2 billion annually (which would be treated as a return on primary education) at a time when only $8 billion was spent on primary education.[10]

Benefits accruing to the future children of the educated come through the informal education which educated parents presumably provide their children. Using data on the additional education that children of more educated parents receive, Weisbrod and Swift have estimated the value in higher earnings of this extra education of the child. They then express these higher earnings of the child as a rate of return to the parents' education. The estimates ranged from 0.25 percent to 8 percent for two-thirds of the cases, and in only about 7 percent of these cases studied was the effect negligible. Even the authors urge caution in use of these estimates.[11]

Education in Consumption

There is one other real potentially quantifiable economic benefit to education, other than the effect on earnings, that has been over-looked frequently, and that is the effect of education on the other side of the individual's financial affairs, the expenditure side. Education not only allows one to earn more income, but should also enable one to spend it more efficiently. The recent rash of consumer protection laws have arisen, in part, because of a recognition of this phenomenon, and because of the increasing complexity of consumer decisions in today's technologically advanced world.

This type of benefit might be called education in consumption as it is analogous to Finis Welch's recently coined phrase "education in production."[12] In trying to answer the question, "With the phenom-enal rise in average education, why have rates of return failed to decline?" Welch proposes and examines empirically for agriculture, the notion that increased education allows a farmer to use his other factors of production more efficiently.[13] Thus education has two effects upon output—the traditional "worker effect" of increasing a factor of production, while holding the others constant (the economist concept of marginal product), and an allocation effect of allowing the worker to combine the other factors of production more efficiently, or perhaps, to use "new factors" that otherwise would not be used. From a study on the effect of education on farmers, Welch found that "much of the 'leverage' associated with added schooling is drawn from the dynamic implications of changing technology."[14] The implications of Welch's findings for rates-of-return analysis are that the rates of return to education should maintain their present level if technological change continues its rapid pace. If technological change slows down, rates of return to education would be likely to fall. Education in production does not bias the rates-of-return analysis because it is simply a factor determining rates of return.

The analogous concept of education in consumption would bias rates of return calculations, because this affects the consumer's expenditure side, not his income side. A search of the literature reveals that this is an unknown phenomenon, and thus the theoretical and empirical work on this topic remains. The idea of education in consumption does logically follow from Welch's pioneering and important study. As consumer buying decisions become more complex with a more technologically advanced environment, the potential saving of income to the educated consumer over the uneducated consumer increases. Rates-of-return analysis that do not allow for this factor (and none have as yet) understate the true internal rate of return. To the extent that educated consumers are more socially minded (for instance, buying the "ecology" soap instead of Tide), the social rate of return to education will be additionally understated.

Externalities

These "externalities" may be regarded initially as effects of goods which, when consumed or produced, either confer benefits or impose costs on persons other than the consumer(s) or producer(s) of those goods. External benefits in consumption, for example, are benefits which contribute to the well-being of people other than the "consumer" himself. To the extent that one person's decisions either benefit or harm others without that person taking into account such benefits or costs, such decisions may lead to underprovision (in the case of external benefits) or overprovision (in the case of external costs), from the social point of view, of the activity involved (and to serious questions about equity).

Economic Externalities

In the case of education, a family may be expected to make decisions based on its expectation of benefits or returns to the family, as these private benefits have been outlined above. And a family would be expected to disregard any benefits or returns conferred on other families. Many economists have pointed out, however, that families other than those of the educated also may benefit from education. This means "social calculation," where *all* private and external benefits are considered.

Again, Weisbrod has been at the forefront in listing categories of such benefits. He mentions the following: (1) residence-related benefits to neighbors and taxpayers, (2) employment-related benefits to fellow workers, and (3) society-related benefits to the population in general. The first two categories contain both social (i.e., noneconomic) and economic externalities and most of the benefits of the third category are social externalities.[b]

Weisbrod first suggests that the education of the children of one family may confer benefits on neighbors by (1) inculcating acceptable social values and behavior norms, (2) providing alternatives to unsupervised activities, some of which may have antisocial consequences, and (3) improving the caliber of voluntary community activities.[15] Also, Weisbrod suggests that benefits are conferred on taxpayers because the need for incurring the "avoidance costs" of law enforcement will tend to be less.

Although these types of benefits will be discussed more thoroughly in the section, "Social Externalities," several observations need to be made here. One global observation is that all that can be said in general is that the effects such as those above undoubtedly have an effect on neighbors, but neither their magnitude nor their direction is clear in any particular instance. For example, the social values children are now taught (from those implicit in sex education to those in what is regarded as the "debunking" of history) are under question and have been challenged seriously by persons outside of the education establishment. Some have even blamed educators for the generation gap. Also, student "unrest" has caused many to wonder if antisocial consequences come only from unsupervised activities. More will be said later on these claims.

Weisbrod suggests that employment-related external benefits

---

[b]Weisbrod also claims, under the residence-related external benefits, the child-care services to mothers and the informal education for future children of the educated. If children were the decisionmakers, these benefits might be considered to be external. Because parents make such decisions, certainly, the first and probably the second are internal to the family, which is the decision-making entity. Only the benefits listed by Weisbrod which seem truly external to the family are discussed here.

are conferred when educating some workers raises the productivity of others.[16] This point requires some elaboration. Production in modern, industrialized economies requires coordination, cooperation, and other interaction of workers, so that the productivity of each worker potentially affects the productivity of every other worker. Additional education of one worker may affect another through emulation of skills and through acquired psychological and motivational factors. Through the simple process of work association, less educated workers may improve their communication and discipline of the mind, develop flexibility and adaptability, and learn maturity and reliability. Through the less simple process of transfer, educated or more educated workers may contribute to the awareness of and the reception to present knowledge and new ideas.[17]

Measurement of employment-related benefits raises problems. "Simply" measuring the higher earnings of a group after more "educated" personnel have been introduced is not so simple. Earnings may not reflect productivity accurately, especially in cases where only *marginal* contributions to output are concerned. Also, it may prove to be difficult to isolate the effects of introduction of educated personnel from other changes which occur simultaneously. Employment-related external benefits, like many other "nonmarket" benefits, are not subject to measurement at this time, and it is therefore infeasible to include them in calculations such as the social rate of return. Actually, we cannot be sure that such effects are always unambiguously positive. O'Donoghue, for example, suggests that the "educational ethos" can be inimical to productivity because it downgrades business and economic activities to a much lower status than cultural, academic, intellectual, artistic, or similar activities.[18]

Finally, Weisbrod discusses external benefits that are conferred on society in general.[19] Democracy hardly is feasible without widespread acceptance of a common set of values and without some minimum degree of citizen literacy and knowledge, so that education might be regarded as providing "a minimum standard of citizenship." Education, it commonly is argued, also is important in promoting equality of opportunity. If education is successful in lowering financial and other barriers to entry into previously privileged positions, then education is providing a return in the form of satisfying a social goal.[20] Measurement of these benefits would be arbitrary, but some aspects of these external benefits of education are discussed further below, particularly the effect of education in poverty reduction, and far more research can be carried out with respect to this distributional element.

Social Externalities

Some writers[21] have commented that an increment of education reduces government expenditures on crime prevention and that it mitigates against poverty, reduces government outlay on fire protection, public health, and medical care. Others have criticized severely the omission of such benefits of education in social rate-of-return studies.[22] While it is still not technically feasible to incorporate all such tradeoffs into benefit-cost analysis, the effects of educational spending on crime and poverty reduction should be examined more carefully.

It should be said at the outset, however, that educational spending may affect the demand for (and supply of) a multitude of other publicly provided goods and services. For example, Shoup asserts the following:

An increment of education reduces government expenditures on crime prevention on balance, though it may increase certain types of crime, embezzlement, for example. It also reduces government outlay on fire protection, public health, and medical care. Education induces an increase in expenditures on highway and streets, and cultural and recreational facilities. It increases tax revenue automatically, after a considerable lapse of time, by increasing productivity and hence, to some degree at least, national income.[23]

The problem with claims of tradeoffs involving education is that of establishing their relative magnitude and even the direction which they take. In other words, do they constitute costs or benefits to others?

Impact on Neighbors and Taxpayers. Weisbrod again has been among the more persistent economists who have argued that education reduces crime. He has argued that "insofar as lack of education leads to employment difficulties and crime, law enforcement costs will tend to be high," and education thus may "provide social benefits by reducing the need for incurring these 'avoidance costs,' to the advantage of taxpayers."[24] Benson, in a similar vein, argues that social values developed through education affect neighbors: "Education has effects on the caliber of voluntary community activities: choral groups, drama clubs, local art shows, etc."[25] This conventional wisdom has been challenged seriously in recent years.

Machlup recently suggested that the experience of the last few years, with student riots and rebellions at universities all over the world, at least should lead to a reconsideration of the assumption which has been taken for granted that education increases respect for law and order and promotes a climate conducive to peaceful social, political, and economic development.[26] E.G. West has suggested that the available data not only fail to support the assertion but, if anything, point to a contrary conclusion.[27]

West points out that in postwar England , crime rates for young people rose rather than fell, despite (or because of) an expansion in education during the period. He cites evidence that the last year of compulsory education was the highest rate of juvenile delinquency, a tendency which was reversed when pupils left school and went to work. When the school-leaving age was raised from thirteen to fourteen in 1947, West claims that "there was an immediate change-over in the delinquency record of the 13-year-olds (who until this had been the most troublesome age groups) and the 14-year-olds, who took their place in 1948, and have held it consistently ever since."[28]

Many comments are in order. West's evidence is owing undoubtedly to compulsion and to the suspicion that the delinquents had no desire to attend school. For older age groups, the external effects on neighbors and taxpayers still may be positive. Even so, many student activities involving their willful desires to do good may not be interpreted as beneficial. O'Donoghue has pointed out that the student riots may be regarded as "good" or "criminal" by different sectors of the same population.[29]

Others have questioned how such activities as voluntary community activities, choral groups, drama clubs, and local art shows may be counted as external benefits of education. In the first place, the activities are largely confined, both for participants and spectators, to educated people and simply represent a form of consumption activity for them. It is not even necessarily true that education confers a benefit by extending the individual's range of consumption activities. As Jack Wiseman has argued, "the graduated student now gets psychic return from having been educated to appreciate

Bach, but he can no longer tolerate the Beatles.''[30] It would be a blatant value judgment to estimate that one consumption activity constituted an improvement over another, thereby conferring a benefit, although it is one that many would be prepared to make.

No one seems to deny, therefore, that education affects neighbors and taxpayers ''externally,'' but there is considerable question as to the value or direction of such effects. By way of generalization, all that can be said at this time is that effects on neighbors and taxpayers are created, but whether they are victims or beneficiaries is not clear in any one instance. Further fruitful research concerning the nature of some of the tradeoffs is certainly called for.

Impact on Poverty Reduction. The traditional belief, of course, is that education tends to equalize the opportunities for financial advancement. The belief that higher levels of education tend to produce a greater equality in the distribution of income is based on the international and interregional studies of Simon Kuznets.[31] Even Paul Samuelson, in his text, *Economics*, makes the statement that both over time and over international cross-sections, equality of the distribution of income increases with per capita income and education.[32] However, increased educational spending hardly is the most direct way to attack the problem of poverty. Ribich points out that a lengthy chain of events must transpire successfully before additional educational spending is reflected in reduced poverty: (1) spending by government must result in augmented educational resources available to schools; (2) the extra resources must add to learning; (3) the additional learning must lead to increases in the capacity to produce and to earn income; and (4) that capability must result in moving individuals out of poverty or at least mitigate the degree of poverty.[33] Between each of these required links between educational spending and poverty reduction, there can be and is slippage.[34]

Ribich has estimated the ''payoff rates'' for several types of educational spending. He found that the ratio of estimated total income gains to costs to be only around 60 percent.[35] Ribich also estimates the effect of inducing a given number of individuals to graduate from high school rather than to drop out. By using a $3,000 income figure as the definition of poverty and by discounting to present values the entire lifetime stream of total income and poverty income tax reductions, he found that (1) the reduction of the poverty income gap is only one-fifth of the total income gain that would be experienced by a representative sample of whites, and (2) the reduction is just short of two-fifths for a representative group of non-whites. (If the income gains were $1 million, then the expected reduction of the poverty income gap would be between $200,000 and $400,000.) If this relationship held for other educational changes as well, it would be valid to reduce the total returns estimates so that the ratio of poverty gap reduction to costs might be no better than 25 percent.[36]

B.R. Chiswick has added importantly to the literature that examines the impact of education on income inequality.[37] Chiswick shows that, other things being equal, a higher level of schooling tends to increase income inequality, but that, because the average level of schooling is negatively correlated with the rate of return and with the inequality of schooling, the observed positive relationship between level of school and income inequality has been maintained.[38] Chiswick explains these findings by pointing out that individuals with greater amounts of education are more likely than people with little education to migrate to states with high education levels, raising them in states with low education levels, causing the negative simple correlation between the average level of education and income inequality.

The implications for policymakers of Chiswick's findings are that it should not be automatically assumed that raising the average level of education will increase the equality of the distribution of income. In fact, the opposite is more likely to result. Two things that should be considered are the way the level of education is raised in a community, that is raising the lower or the upper tail of the distribution of the years of education, and second, the effect of increasing the level of education on rates of return. Usually one expects that increasing the level of education will lower the rates of return, but in some cases, the resulting increased incomes and economic growth might generate more than enough demand for skilled labor to offset the increase in supply. This occurrence is probably more likely for underdeveloped countries than for the United States.

Edward Denison has criticized the idea that the United States educational structure promotes equality of opportunity and income.[39] Denison is mainly criticizing United States higher education when he claims that equality of opportunity requires expenditures on dull students at least as great as the expenditures on bright students. Yet Denison calculates that the average expenditure of public funds for four years of college on male students who had an A average in high school is $5,811, while the corresponding figure for males and females with a below C− average is $666 and zero, respectively.[40] Public subsidization of ability obviously increases income inequality, because incomes and ability are already highly correlated. These criticisms also apply to primary and secondary schools that allocate more funds and better teachers to honors programs or even college preparatory programs.

If promoting a more equal distribution of income is a societal goal, there may well be a tradeoff between equity and allocative efficiency. Clearly, educating students with more ability more intensely will result in higher rates of return. In a democratic society, the people must decide on this tradeoff through the political process, while the role of the economist is to attempt to quantify the tradeoff and present it to the people. Much work remains to be completed here.

Not all the policy implications of these various studies on the distributional impact of educational investment are (assuming that it is a goal of society to have a more equitable distribution of income) in conflict with the dictates of rate-of-return analysis. Indeed, in most respects, the equity and allocative considerations reinforce each other, especially with regard to investment in the different levels of schooling. Both Chiswick and Denison would recommend that public educational funds should be reallocated from higher to lower levels of education to increase income equality. This, of course, is the same conclusion that the evidence from rate-of-return studies indicates should be undertaken to increase the allocative efficiency of educational investment.

Attempting benefit-cost analysis of alternative government actions often means provision of data regarding costs and gains without any markets to generate the information. It is agreed, generally, that it is as often infinitely expensive, that is, impossible to provide information about marginal evaluations that is comparable in quality to the knowledge generated by markets.[41] This means that many social benefits and costs go unmeasured in studies of education and other services characterized by some degree of externalities which are "unpriced and uncosted." Nonetheless, benefit-cost analysis can be of use in studying services such as education. For one thing, benefit-cost analysis can provide *some* information, and it can alert officials and citizens to look at education as a problem of *choice*, even if many of the quantities and values must be filled in on the basis of judgment.[42] But at least it can focus the attention of the policymaker upon the proper matrix.

Geographic Spillovers. Weisbrod's most controversial conclusions probably have been those with regard to geographic spillovers. His study[43] and that of Hirsch et al.,[44] are based on the idea that education may bring benefits to people other than those in *the school district* which provides the education[c]. Weisbrod's main hypothesis is that migration gives rise to spillovers because the costs of education are borne by the emigrant area and that such spillovers result in underinvestment in education. In other words, he argues that one of the consequences of *federalism* is that the level of educational provision will fall short of the social optimum. For example, a community might not devote $1,000 of resources to produce an output worth $1,300 to society if only $800 of benefits accrue to persons within the school district. Not only would a community disregard any "spillout" benefits, but any "spillin" benefits as well. To continue the example, a community might not devote the $1,000 of resources even if there were $600 of spillin benefits, more than enough to offset the $500 of spillout benefits. His theory is that a community will extend the provision of education only to the point where the *marginal* benefits to the community equal its *marginal* costs, disregarding any benefits which accrue to other areas (for obvious reasons) and disregarding spillin benefits because they constitute a type of *lump-sum* benefit which have no influence on *marginal* decisions to either raise or lower the level of provision within the community.[45]

Weisbrod's hypothesis that geographic spillovers lead to global underinvestment in education has been criticized widely. Malul was critical of his use of data.[46] Holtmann argued that under Weisbrod's circumstances, no community would provide "free" education and that migration is not a cause of nonoptimal provision of education.[47]

---

[c]Whatever these "spillovers" are, some argue they are not externalities. Shoup has called these simply "a geographical concept involving only one service at a time, a service or disservice—rendered over an area only part of which is within the boundaries of a political group, that is, within the boundaries of the governmental unit that decides upon and dispenses the service." Shoup, *Public Finance*. Weisbrod, nonetheless, refers to benefits accruing inside the school district as "internal" benefits and those accruing to persons outside the district as "external" benefits.

Williams submitted that in some cases (when spillins are taken into account), suboptimality will be greater than Weisbrod has estimated, and in other cases, too much of education will be provided.[48]

As it is with other discussions of the nonmarket benefits (and costs), the effect of geographic spillovers on the level of provision of education is unclear. We are certain neither of the extent nor of the direction which any such effects might take. Certainly, federalism has some effect on the provision of education. For example, drawing geographic distinctions may serve in many cases to make "indirect" benefits seem more remote than they really are, thereby mitigating an interest one otherwise might have in the education of the children of other families. Also, dividing sovereignty among myriad units of government makes interference in the decisions of others more difficult, even where one group of citizens has a strong interest (for whatever reasons) in seeing that children in another state or locality are educated better than they actually are being educated.[49]

Externalities and Resource Allocation

Whether it is water pollution and smog (cases of external cost and overprovision) or education, a fundamental question raised about externalities is in regard to the effects of consumption or production on persons other than the parties to an exchange. Without some kind of adjustment (such as prohibition, directive, bribery, merger, taxes and subsidies, or regulation[50]), the economy may either overprovide (in the case of external costs) or underprovide (in the case of external benefits) goods and services characterized by externality, at least when judged from the social point of view. The problem of socially efficient and socially equitable provision of education is then twofold: (1) some adjustment must be made to extend expenditures beyond the socially suboptimal level associated with regard only for the private benefit of education to a level approximating that associated with regard for all the benefits—private and external—of education, and (2) some means must be applied to distribute the costs of the socially optimal level of education according to commonly embraced norms of social justice. The traditional solutions for efficient provision of goods characterized by external benefits are (1) to establish minimum standards of performance, (2) to subsidize the producer or consumer of the good, and (3) to enlarge the decision-making unit so as to "internalize" the benefits.

Minimum Standards. The idea of minimum standards is to require consumers to purchase quantities larger than they would if left to their own choice. In the case of education, families might "purchase" less than the socially optimal amount of education for their children if left to their own choice. This traditional solution would prescribe that families be required to provide each of their children with a certain number of student-years of education. Some kind of subsidy almost certainly must be involved with such a requirement, however. Individuals who genuinely cannot pay the costs of meeting required standards could not be asked to divest themselves of their children by selling them to others who can, which is what we do when owners cannot afford to raise buildings, automobiles, and other property to minimum standards.

Subsidies. The idea of subsidies is to reduce the cost of such goods to consumers (or producers) and thereby to increase their consumption (or production). By reducing the cost of education, for example, it is hoped that families may respond by consuming a larger (than otherwise) quantity. There is widespread agreement that subsidies and minimum standard of performance are necessary to provide education optimally from the social point of view. The disagreement is over such questions as (1) what should be the level of subsidy, (2) should producers or consumers be subsidized, (3) should the subsidy be selective or "across the board," and (4) what should be the tax base of the subsidy?

First, we really cannot expect people to reveal their demand or willingness to pay for the external benefits of education. This component of education is what economists call "public," meaning that the consumption of the external benefits by one person does not diminish the opportunity of others to consume the same benefits. Put another way, families other than those of the educated must all adjust to the same quantity of the public component of education—more of the public component of education for one of these other families is more for them all. Under such conditions, each of the "other" families may decide not to reveal its willingness to pay for any benefit provided to it externally on the grounds that it can enjoy whatever external benefits which are forthcoming whether or not it contributes toward the provision of those external benefits. Because of this problem of concealed "preferences," we really cannot know by how much to extend by subsidy the level of educational spending. One of the consequences of moving away from what is regarded as a suboptimal level of provision by means of a subsidy, therefore, might be to end up by overproviding education. The optimal level of subsidy, in any event, is indeterminate because of the indeterminary of the total demand for education.

Even if we could determine the optimal level of subsidy, this would not resolve the question of whether to subsidize producers or consumers. Presently, of course, we subsidize the producers of education to the extent that education is offered at a price of practically zero to consumers. An alternative would be to subsidize the consumers in the form of "market-type vouchers" and to allow the market price of education to be determined by competition between rival schools. This proposal[51] has not yet been studied fully, but many have expressed reservations based on uncertainty about the effect of monopoly, particularly in small communities, unwillingness to allow "ignorant" families to exercise consumer sovereignty, and questions about the possible effects on academic freedom.

Since one purpose of subsidies is to satisfy the privately disregarded external benefits, selective subsidization might be preferred over across-the-board subsidization. For example, areas of study closely connected with citizen quality could be singled out for subsidy, or subsidies might take the form of cash support of youths who otherwise would drop out of programs, since it is such students at whom meeting such objectives is commonly aimed.[52] Selective subsidies have been used in principle, but the consequences of wider or more detailed use have not been explored carefully.

Finally, what base should be used to defray the cost of the subsidy? Subsidies to primary and secondary education usually are defrayed by the property tax. Because the burden of property taxes typically is distributed regressively over income groups, however, there is an obvious paradox: on one hand, we express an interest in education as a means of reducing inequality of opportunity, while, on the other hand, we finance education in a way which makes income distribution more unequal, thereby making the problem of reducing inequality of opportunity all the more difficult. There are other problems with the choice of tax base. If it is acquiescence we want in moving from a lower to a higher level of provision of education, then the more likely we are to get it as an individual's proportion of the base, other things equal, moves toward a minimum. In other words, we are more likely to gain acquiescence in extending the provision of education if the statewide sales base is used rather than the local property base, the national income base rather than the statewide sales base, and so forth.

Internalization. The very word *externality* seems to lead naturally and logically to "internalization" as a solution. Internalization refers to enlarging the decision-making unit until its size corresponds with the spillover of benefits (or costs). In other words, if some benefits remain outside when decisions are made by an individual or group, then cannot the benefits be brought inside if we increase the size of the decision-making unit? In cases involving individuals, the answer is no. For example, in the case of education, benefits are external to the family, and we cannot increase the size of the family until it is large enough to "capture" all of the benefits. Internalization, when it has been proposed as a "cure-all" for what ails education, has been advanced mostly out of mistaking "geographical spillovers" for externalities.

Conditions for Optimal Provision of Education

By treating education variously as a neighborhood effect, a spillover, an externality, and more recently, as a good with both a public and a private component, the conditions for optimal provision of education have been confused. Mark Pauly[53] expressed the optimality conditions for education by treating it as a consumption externality in the Buchanan-Stubblebine[54] tradition. By rearranging the Buchanan-Stubblebine-Pauly equilibrium solution, however, one obtains Samuelson's equation for optimal provision of a pure public good.[55] This is unsatisfactory because education contains obvious elements of a private-good nature.

Mathematically, we can derive (see Appendix 2A) the optimality condition for education as a good with a private and public component in joint supply. For a pair of goods x_{n+m+1} (private) and x_{n+m+2} (public), supplied in fixed proportion, the necessary condition is

$$\frac{U^i_{n+m+1}}{u^i_r} + \sum_{i=1}^{s} \frac{U^i_{n+m+2}}{U^i_r} = \frac{F_{n+m+1}}{F_r} \qquad (2.1)$$

where, for example, U^i_{n+m+1} is the marginal utility of the $(n+m+1)^{th}$

good for the ith individual and F_{n+m+1}/F_r is the marginal rate of transformation between good $n+m+1$ and numeraire private good r.

Graphically, the market demand curve for the private component of such a good may be derived by summing *horizontally* the demand curves of individuals. The "pseudo-demand curve" for the public component is obtained by summing *vertically* the pseudo-demand curves of individuals. Then, because they are joint products, total demand is obtained by summing *vertically* over components. The two vertical summations are required for different reasons. The former is because of publicness, that is, jointness of supply, and is over individuals; the latter is because of joint supply and is over goods, or in this case, components.[56]

The optimality conditions for education are shown in Figure 2-2. The demand curves D_1, D_2, and D_3 are for families 1, 2, and 3 who are assumed to have one school-age child each. D_m is the horizontally summed market demand curves of the three families for student-years of education. Demand curves D_a, D_b, D_c are for families a, b, and c—which may or may not be the same families as 1, 2, and 3—who are beneficiaries of education of other families' children. Because of the jointness of supply, these demand curves can be summed vertically to derive the total demand curve for the public component and then, because of the joint supply of a private and public component, summed vertically with D_m to derive the combined demand curve for education, which is $D_m + D_t$ in Figure 2-2. Assuming constant marginal cost, the optimal quantity of education is OQ_e student-years. The market price paid by each of the three families is P_m, and each student-year of education is subsidized by family b in the amount of P_b and by family c in the amount of P_c. The sum of P_m, P_b, and P_c is just sufficient to cover the marginal cost of a student-year of education. Finally, family 1 will consume Q_1 student-years, family 2 will consume Q_2 and family 3 will consume Q_3. This graphic depiction of an algorithm which satisfies the optimality conditions for education applies only if student-years of education are homogenous, that is, families a, b, and c are indifferent to the distribution of student-years among children of families 1, 2, and 3.

In Figure 2-3, we drop this assumption. Because of community interest in equality of opportunity, for example, it may place a higher value on a student-year of education for children of low-income families than for children of median- or high-income families. In

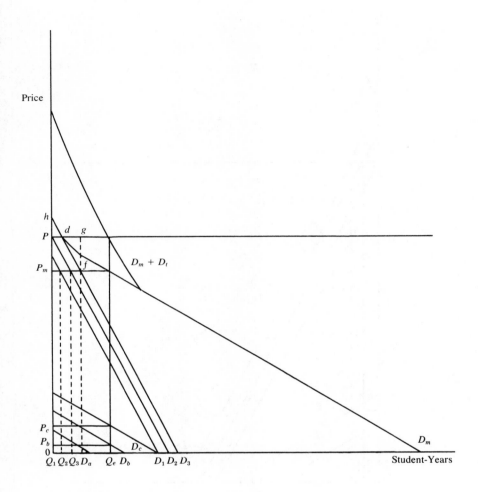

Figure 2-2. Optimality: Partial Equilibrium with Homogeneous Student-years of Education

Figure 2-3, therefore, we assume that families 1, 2, and 3 have different incomes and that education is a normal good. The community demand curves D_a, D_b, and D_c are for student-years consumed by the children of families of 3, 2, and 1, respectively. Because of jointness of supply, these community demand curves are the result of vertical summation over individual demand curves.

Again, we have a case of joint supply: there is a private and a public component of education, and we can sum the two compo-

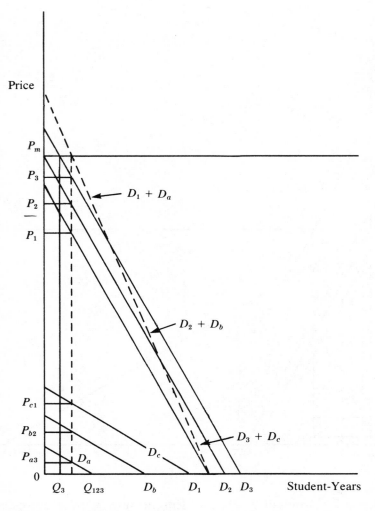

Figure 2-3. Optimality: Partial Equilibrium with Heterogeneous Student-years of Education

nents vertically in order to get the combined demand for the production unit, that is, a year of education. Because of the geometric construction of the figure, the combined demand curve for the education of each family's children lies along the same locus, thereby giving the appearance of a single curve, whereas there are in fact three separate curves. Satisfaction of the optimality condition of our equation requires a subsidy of P_{a3} to family 3, P_{b2} to family 2, and P_{c1} to family 1. This has the effect of reducing the price paid for a student-year of education to P_3 to family 3, P_2 to family 2, and P_1 to family 1. Whereas only family 3 purchases any education (Q_3 units) in the absence of subsidies, in our example all three families purchase the same amount, Q_{123}, with differential subsidies.

Conclusion on Externalities

The more difficult component of benefits to measure or even to identify is the category of benefits that accrue not to the family of the educated but rather to other families. To reiterate, such effects are called "externalities," "neighborhood effects," "spillovers," and a variety of other labels. Their nature is to affect the production or consumption activities of others. For example, recall that education may confer external benefits in the following ways: (1) neighbors may benefit because children have fewer hours of unsupervised activities, some of which are likely to affect them adversely; (2) taxpayers may benefit because education may lead to reduced unemployment, poverty, and crime, the consequences of which involve costs to some extent borne by them; and (3) society at large may benefit because of effects such as that which literacy has on the functioning of a market economy and of a political democracy. Such benefits may be regarded as "social" rather than private in nature; and such wider consequences of education would be relevant to any decisions on educational spending.

These social externalities of education include such things as providing the necessary conditions for a smoothly functioning democracy, inculcating new generations with the traditions and accepted values of society, and perhaps promoting equality of opportunity through lower job barriers based on class, racial, and religious grounds. To be complete, some possible social external diseconomies of education should be enumerated. Recent events indicate that education beyond a certain point leads to a questioning of the social, religious, and political beliefs of a society. This makes it harder to govern that society, and democracy may change to anarchy. From the point of view of the existing majority of society, this type of externality is a social cost. In a long-run broad social sense, however, it is not clear whether this externality is a cost or a benefit. To the policymakers currently in power, it must be counted as a social cost.

On the benefits side, the above analysis indicates that the total benefits will be understated by the reference only to the private benefits, and that a public means of support for education is therefore justified. This conclusion is further reinforced when it is noted that private benefits are usually calculated net of personal income taxes. The social return should, of course, include taxes paid to society. The other major reasons for the conclusion that the calculated private benefits understate the social benefits to education, are the probable importance of education in reducing the real cost of consumption (the education in consumption proposal). The understatement is also likely to diminish with increasing years of education. This is most clear with the externality argument, especially, because some externalities may become negative at a high enough level of education. Also, the babysitting benefit to mothers is likely to be more important at lower levels of education. This might not be true, however, for the education in consumption hypothesis, because a threshold level of a college education may be required for consumers to appreciably save on the expenditure side while maintaining the same real value of consumer goods as less educated consumers.[d] Further research needs to be done on this question.

On the cost side, to the extent that the government pays for part of the educational costs, the private costs will understate the social costs. Because opportunity costs and private direct costs rise relative to the direct costs paid by the state as the grade of schooling rises from 1 to 12—or 14, if there are junior community colleges—private costs will understate social costs by a decreasing amount as the level of schooling increases.

The net effect of the two offsetting biases of the cost side and the benefit side is probably to continue to cause the internal rate of return (which is not calculated to include the benefits of education in consumption) to understate the true social rate of return that includes the social and economic externalities. There is no way to support this statement empirically as yet, and indeed, some economists—Schultz, for example—assume that the internal and

---

[d]Welch found that there was no education in production effect for high school graduates in farming while there was a significant effect for college graduates. Welch, ''Education in Production,'' p. 55.

the social rates of return are identical. A stronger statement can be made about the relative rates of return biases for different years of education. Most of the biases on both the cost and the benefit sides run in the direction of the internal rate of return underestimating the social rate of return by a decreasing amount with further education. The conclusions are not that void of policy significance because most of the decisions in educational finance will probably be made in allocating a fixed amount of funds allotted to education to the different types of education—primary, secondary, junior college, or higher education—rather than the actual amount to be allotted to all types of education. However, the latter is an important question also and can be answered with rates-of-return analysis although with less confidence than the intraeducational allocative questions.

Appendix 2A

The Equation (2.1) on page 27 may be derived as follows: For simplicity, assume two individuals, indicated by superscripts 1, 2; a private good x_1 and a public good x_2 in joint supply; and a purely private good x_r.

Maximize $\qquad\qquad\qquad u^1(x_1^1, x_2, x_r^1)$ $\qquad\qquad\qquad$ (2A.1)

subject to $\qquad\qquad\quad u^2(x_1^2, x_2, x_r^2) = u^{-2}$ $\qquad\qquad$ (2A.2)

$$x_1^1 + x_1^2 = x_1 \qquad\qquad (2A.3)$$

$$x_1 = x_2 \qquad\qquad (2A.4)$$

$$x_r^1 + x_r^2 = x_r \qquad\qquad (2A.5)$$

and

$$F(x_1, x_r) = 0 \qquad\qquad (2A.6)$$

The Lagrangian is

$$L = u^1(x_1^1, x_2, x_r^1) + \lambda_1[u^2(x_1^2, x_2, x_2^2)] \qquad (2A.7)$$
$$+ \lambda_2(x_1^1 + x_1^2 - x_1) + \lambda_3(x_1, - x_2) + \lambda_4 F(x_1, x_r).$$

Setting the partial derivatives equal to zero,

$$u_1^1 + \lambda_2 + 0 \qquad\qquad (2A.8)$$

$$\lambda_1 u_1 + \lambda_2 = 0 \qquad\qquad (2A.9)$$

$$-\lambda_2 + \lambda_3 + \lambda_4 F_1 = 0 \qquad\qquad (2A.10)$$

$$u_2^1 + \lambda_1 u_2^2 - \lambda_3 = 0 \qquad\qquad (2A.11)$$

$$u_r^1 + \lambda_4 F_r = 0 \qquad\qquad (2A.12)$$

$$\lambda_1 u_r^2 + \lambda_4 F_r + 0 \qquad\qquad (2A.13)$$

which yields

$$\frac{u_1^1}{u_r^1} + \frac{u_2^1}{u_r^1} + \frac{u_1^1 u_2^2}{u_r^1 u_1^2} = \frac{F_1}{F_r} \qquad\qquad (2A.14)$$

But from (2A.14) and (2A.13)

$$\frac{u_1^1}{u_r^1} = \frac{u_1^2}{u_r^2} . \qquad\qquad (2A.15)$$

35

Therefore

$$\frac{u_1^1}{u_r^1} + \frac{u_2^1}{u_r^2} + \frac{u_2^2}{u_r^2} = \frac{F_1}{F_2} \tag{2A.16}$$

or

$$\frac{u_1^1}{u_r^1} + \sum_{i=1}^{2} \frac{u_2^i}{u_r} = \frac{F_1}{F_r}, \tag{2A.17}$$

which is equivalent to equation (2.1).

3 Educational Investment and the Valuation Problem

Evaluating Educational Investment

The economist's theory of human capital gives him the analytical tools to arrive at some insights, not only about the relative amount of investment in education vis-á-vis other forms of investment, but also about the allocation of investment funds among different types of education. The instruments we are speaking of are benefit-cost analysis (and its modern offshoots) and rate-of-return analysis.

Benefit-Cost Analysis

Benefit-cost analysis is simply an attempt to identify and to measure the benefits and costs that would result from alternative courses of action. As such, the idea hardly is a new one—presumably, man always has weighed the pros and cons, the advantages and disadvantages, of alternative actions. But techniques have been improved and refined (almost beyond recognition, in some cases) until now we have different names for some of the different applications of benefit-cost analysis: when courses of action are in national defense planning, it is called "cost-effectiveness analysis"; when the alternatives are relatively complex collections of interrelated parts, it is called "systems analysis"; and when the alternatives are modes of operations with given resources, it is called "operations research."[1]

Originally, the term and concept "benefit-cost analysis" was associated with, and applied to, natural resource projects, but its most popularized use probably has been in national defense planning. In the late 1940s, the Rand Corporation used "costing" methods in determining for the U.S. Air Force the best strategic bomber for development and next generation use. During the 1950s, however, full-fledged cost-benefit analysis was used widely for the first time in water resource studies.[2] At about the same time, Charles J. Hitch and Roland N. McKean published a highly influential book[3]

37

on efficiency in defense economics which signalled the beginning of a new era of economic analysis applied to the public sector.

Hitch and McKean suggested that economic analysis of military planning involved a comparison of relevant alternatives in terms of the objectives and costs of each, and selection of the best alternative through the application of an appropriate preferredness criterion. In 1961, after Hitch had become comptroller of the Department of Defense, the defense establishment adopted costing methods, and the techniques which became known as "PPBS" (planning-programming-budgeting system) and "program packaging" were underway. By 1965, more than twenty-five agencies of the federal government were using this approach to some extent.

Recently, applications of the benefit-cost principle have become more and more imaginative as comparisons have been made of among other things, alternative health measures, transportation systems, antipoverty proposals, and educational practices.[4] Regardless of the applications, however, the role of the benefit-cost analysis remains the same—it explicitly compares the estimated benefits of an action (or of no action) with what taking action (or no action) costs, at least as long as its use is limited to cases where "what is realized (the benefits) can be expressed in the same units as what is sacrificed in alternatives (the costs)."[5]

In any application, moreover, benefit-cost analysis has certain common elements. It involves the following: (1) the programs, goals, objectives, targets, or beneficial things to be achieved must be identified; (2) the feasible arrangements or systems for meeting these objectives must be identified; (3) the costs of each alternative, or the benefits foregone if one of the alternatives is adopted, must be identified and measured; (4) models must be developed which help to trace out the impact of each alternative on achievements (i.e., on benefits) or costs; and (5) a criterion, involving both costs and benefits, must be developed which appropriately identifies the preferred alternative.[6] The first four steps, therefore, are the process of identifying and measuring the benefits and costs of feasible alternatives and the final step is the choice mechanism which selects the "best" alternative.

Benefit-Cost Studies of Educational Programs

As a technique and methodology of evaluation, benefit-cost analysis has been used increasingly in the 1960s and 1970s to judge the effectiveness of educational programs. Four types of programs in particular have been evaluated: (1) job retraining, (2) dropout prevention, (3) compensatory education, and (4) preschool programs for culturally deprived children.[7]

Job Retraining. Retraining courses for adult workers were provided for under the Area Redevelopment Act (ARA-1961) and the Manpower Development and Training Act (MDTA-1962), both of which were part of the War on Poverty. Evaluations were made of retraining courses in West Virginia by Gibbard and Somers,[8] Cain and Stromsdorfer,[9] Somers and Stromsdorfer,[10] and Stromsdorfer;[11] in Tennessee by Solie;[12] in Connecticut by Borus;[13] in Massachusetts by Page,[14] and Gooding;[15] in Michigan by Hardin and Borus;[16] and Main[17] has evaluated the MDTA in a nationwide study. In most of these evaluations, time-discounted gains in before-tax earnings[a] are compared to training costs.

All of these studies basically come to the same conclusions: the gain in earnings exceeds the cost of retraining, meaning that retraining is more effective than a simple transfer of income. The benefit-cost ratio ranges from about five to fifteen. Some of the results are shown in Table 3-1, but readers must be warned that discount rates ranging from 4 to 10 percent were applied to earnings. In any event, the evidence seems to indicate that job retraining is a "profitable" social undertaking.

However, a closer look at those results leads one to a more agnostic position. Earl Main, who probably paid the closest attention to the methodological problems that arise, appended a cautious note to his favorable findings. Main's study is based on a nationwide sample of 1,200 trainees and a sample of 1,000 persons who were unemployed at about the same time the training started. A multiple regression equation was used to control for factors other than the training that might effect wages and employment and that differed between the groups. Main concluded that a year after the completion of the training, the trainee group did attain a higher level of employment, but not better paying jobs than the nontrainee group.[18] However, Main qualified this conclusion with the warning that such factors as motivation and intelligence (which were not controlled) may explain the higher employment opportunities of the trainee group.[19]

---

[a]The usual technique is to rely on surveys taken one year after retraining and to extrapolate.

Table 3-1
Estimates of Benefit-Cost Ratios for Retraining Programs in Three States

Study	B-C Ratio
Connecticut	
Borus	73.3-137.3[a]
Ribich[b]	10.1
Hardin[c]	5.9-14.5
Massachusetts	
Page	6.1
Ribich[d]	4.2
Hardin[e]	3.9
West Virginia	
Somers and Stromsdorfer	12.9
Ribich[f]	15.0
Cain and Stromsdorfer	
Men	10.5
Women	2.7
Both sexes	9.3
Hardin[g]	
Men	6.7
Women	2.2
Both sexes	5.7

[a]Depends on assumptions concerning use of skills learned in the course.

[b]Borus's estimate adjusted by Ribich, *Education and Poverty,* p. 49. Borus inappropriately applied a national income multiplier to the estimated gain in earnings.

[c]Borus's estimate adjusted by Einar Hardin, "Benefit-Cost Analyses of Occupational Training Programs: A Comparison of Recent Studies," *Cost Benefit Analysis of Manpower Policies,* eds., G. G. Somers and W. D. Wood (Kingston, Ontario: Industrial Relations Centre, Queen's University, 1969), p. 113.

[d]Page's estimate adjusted by Ribich, *Education and Poverty.*

[e]Page's estimate adjusted by Hardin, "Benefit-Cost Analyses."

[f]Somer's and Stromsdorfer's estimate adjusted by Ribich, *Education and Poverty.*

[g]Cain's and Stromsdorfer's estimate adjusted by Hardin, "Benefit-Cost Analysis."

In a review of Main's study as well as other MDTA evaluations, Robert Hall found additional biases in the selection of the comparison group that tend to work in favor of the program. He states: "Even a well-conceived and executed study such as Main's does not make a convincing case that training programs affect unemployment at all."[20]

Several other problems with such studies should also be mentioned. First, there may be a displacement effect on other unskilled workers. Although this phenomenon does not affect the "private" benefit-cost ratio, it does lower the more relevant social benefit-cost ratio. The effect of the program on the income and welfare of nonparticipants should be taken into account. Second, there is reason to believe from the experiences of other programs that the observed effect on earnings may be short-lived. A study by Ashenfelter using longitudinal social security data found that the absolute earnings differential between MDTA graduates and a comparison group did decline over time.[21] Also, the fact that on-the-job training programs tend to show better results than institutional training may be due to the immediate employment effects of counseling and job placement services rather than from the increased skills learned from the programs.[22]

Dropout Prevention. Such educational programs as the Job Corps and the Neighborhood Youth Corps concentrate on the problems of underemployment and unemployment among disadvantaged youth. The Job Corps was cut back drastically by the Nixon administration on grounds that it was too costly and ineffective, a judgment which was made on the basis of a study prepared for the General Accounting Office by the Resource Management Corporation.[23]

Typical payoffs and costs of dropout prevention programs are not as straightforward as in the case of job-retraining programs. Weisbrod[24] evaluated a St. Louis program in 1960-1962 when work orientation was not emphasized as much as the Job Corps or in the Neighborhood Youth Corps. His estimates, shown as adjusted by Ribich in Table 3-2, showed that costs—estimated to be $8,200 per prevented dropout—exceeded benefits. Almost from the very beginning of evaluating such programs, therefore, there was some measure of doubt regarding the payoff for not dropping out of high school.

Somers and Stromsdorfer studied 60 randomly selected in-school and summer Neighborhood Youth Corps projects out of the 1120 that operated in 1965 to 1967.[25] They concluded that the combined programs did provide significant monetary gains to the participants and therefore were socially efficient. However, the benefits were due mainly to an increased labor-force participation rate and not to any reduction in the dropout rate.

Recent studies have evaluated the Job Corps itself. Cain[26] studied the educational gains and initial placement in the Job Corps. He estimated the benefit-cost ratios at 1.2 to 1 for both the educational gain and the placement data. Cain used "no-shows," that is, those who signed up for the Job Corps but failed to enroll, as the

Table 3-2
Benefit-Cost Estimates of St. Louis Dropout Prevention Programs,
Based on Selected Income Streams[a]

Income Stream	Financial Value of Not Dropping Out of High School[b]	Benefit-lost Ratio at Cost of $8,200 per Prevented Dropout
1949 Median Income, North and West	$3,427	0.42
1959 Median Income, Central Cities	5,261	0.64
1959 Mean Earnings, North and West	5,673	0.69

[a]Estimated by Ribich, *Education and Poverty*, p. 56, and based on estimates of Weisbrod, "Preventing High School Dropout."
[b]Lifetime differences between high school dropouts and graduates, adjusted for mortality rates with retirement assumed to take place at age sixty-five and discounted by 5 percent.

control group for the placement portion and cohort data for the educational gain portion.[27] Results of a study by Levitan[28] also concluded that, although the costs of the Job Corps are high, the benefits of the program are sufficient to justify them. Also, a study by the Job Corps, itself, estimated the benefit-cost ratio between 2:1 and 5:1.

Using the same data, however, the influential RMC evaluation estimated the benefit-cost ratio at only 0.3:1, and a GAO study showed that those who completed the Job Corps had approximately the same wage and unemployment rate as the no-shows. The no-shows began with higher wage rates, however, and if a before-and-after comparison was made for both groups, the Job Corps appears to be more effective than admitted by RMC and GAO. Also, the GAO-RMC studies have been criticized because they are inadequate for reliable in-depth cost-benefit analysis and because they failed to distinguish between urban and conservation centers, for which different rates of return probably hold.[29]

Also, the cost estimates of most of these studies have been over-estimated because the savings in income transfers that would have been paid out to these youths had they not been in the program were not counted. Furthermore, the Job Corps, unlike the other programs, does concentrate entirely on the most disadvantaged youths.[30] Some credit should be given to the equity aspects of this program.

Table 3-3
Estimates of Benefits and Costs for Higher Horizons Program

Item	Elementary School	Junior High School
1. Present value of one year of extra schooling[a]	$2,410	$2,838
2. Average percentage of year gained as result of program[b]	3%	3.3%
3. Benefit per student (line 1 × line 2)	$ 72	$ 94
4. Number of school years between tests	2.00	1.75
5. Cost per student at $61 per year (line 4 × $61)	$ 122	$ 107
6. Benefit-cost ratio (Line 3 ÷ line 5)	0.59	0.88

[a]Figures based on difference in 1959 mean earnings between graduates and dropouts between the ages of eighteen and sixty-five.
[b]Based on averages for reading and quantitative achievement tests.

Compensatory Education. Compensatory education programs began in the late 1950s and were reinforced by grants under Title I of the Elementary and Secondary Act of 1965. Generally, the programs provide supplementary educational services to children culturally deprived because of poverty, low educational attainment of parents, large family size, broken homes, discrimination, and slum conditions. Ribich[31] has evaluated six such programs, but the Higher Horizons Program in New York City provided him with his most reliable results.

Higher Horizons started in 1959, and inaugurated special services, including remedial reading, extra counseling, cultural activities, and special curriculum. Ribich found that the benefit-cost ratios for Higher Horizons were not much different from those for dropout prevention programs. For both the elementary and the junior high levels, the benefit-cost ratio is less than unity. Financial gains at the junior high school level are about 90 percent of costs, but only about 60 percent for the elementary school level. Ribich's evaluations are shown in Table 3-3.

Ribich also evaluated several other programs, all of which took place in large urban areas outside the Deep South. In three of the programs, control groups scored slightly higher on standardized tests than the children receiving compensatory education did. The

Table 3-4
Estimates of Benefits and Costs for Compensatory Education Programs in Five Large Urban Areas Outside the South

	Program	
Item	*A*	*B*
1. Present value of one year of extra schooling[a]	$2,308	$2,093-$2,733
2. Average percentage of year gained as result of program[b]	7%	33%
3. Benefit per student (line 1 × line 2)	$ 162	$690-$902
4. Cost per student	$ 114	$ 160
5. Benefit-cost ratio (line 3 ÷ line 4)	1.4	4.3-5.6

[a]Based on difference in 1959 mean earnings between graduates and dropouts between the ages of eighteen and sixty-five.
[b]Based on yearly equivalent mean scores of experimental and control groups.

difference in mean scores was not statistically significant, however.[32] In a fourth program, cross-sectional comparisons showed that children in compensatory programs learned more between the early and later grades. For still another program consisting of a summer school for underprivileged pupils, a positive effect on achievement also was found, although there was no formal control group. The benefits of the latter two programs were estimated by Ribich to be about 1.5 to 6 times costs. These results are shown in Table 3-4. Even Ribich cautions, however, that "the links constructed between test score gains and future income are not very strong."[33]

Several other major evaluations of compensatory education programs have recently been completed with similar discouraging findings. One study that examined test scores in fourteen large cities before and after the application of Title I funding discovered that average test scores declined slightly.[34] However, Rivlin points to this study more for its illustration of the methodological difficulties one encounters when national evaluations of compensatory programs are attempted than for the significance of the findings.[35] Rivlin points out that Title I was not designed to produce scientifically reliable evaluative information. Each school system gathered different types of data, used different tests and, in general, did not follow the proper evaluative procedures.

Another survey found that only 40 of 1,200 compensatory education programs funded by the Office of Education produced significant gains in achievement.[36] Turning to private business may not be the answer either, according to a study of Garfinkel and Gramlich on performance contracting.[37] They evaluated the OEO experiment on performance contracting for disadvantaged students that was run in eighteen school districts with six different firms. Control groups were carefully selected and the tests used for the evaluation were different from the ones used to determine the payments to the firms. This procedure was used in order to control for the "teaching for the test effect." Garfinkel and Gramlich conclude:

This evidence indicates with surprising uniformity that the performance contractors who participated in the experiment do not currently have the capability of bringing about any great improvement in the educational status of disadvantaged children.[38]

Preschool Programs. Headstart programs were founded on the premise that the time to compensate for cultural deprivation is prior to the school years. The first of these programs was with four-year-old slum children, who were tested at the start of nursery school and again at the end of kindergarten. The Stanford-Benet Intelligence Scale showed a gain of twelve I.Q. points, but the Columbia Mental Maturity Scale showed a slightly lower, statistically insignificant, score for the experimental group as compared to the control group.

In his evaluation of this program, Ribich averaged the two test results to assess the economic gain of the I.Q. gains. He assumed that six points of higher I.Q. was equivalent to 0.7 of a year of extra achievement. Ribich estimated that the value of the program was $1,395 when discounted to age four. Net expenditures per pupil were $2,400, however. The benefit-cost ratio, therefore, was only 0.58.[39]

Summary

Most of the recent methodologically sound studies using proper control groups and longitudinal data have given the special education programs evaluated low benefit-cost marks. The finding is particularly true for programs targeted at the disadvantaged. These results are somewhat in contrast to the earliest attempts at benefit-cost analyses of educational programs. There are several ways to react to these findings. One is to shift emphasis from the efficiency to the equity criterion and to put more stock into the nonquantifiable social benefits belief. Another is to call for "systematic social experimentation" and to point to the previous educational programs as examples of social programs with built-in biases against evaluation.[40] Perhaps the programs were not innovative enough or perhaps the successes of some programs have been inundated by the failures of the majority.

Along these lines and despite the failure of performance contracting, some social scientists see the answer in the private market. Educational vouchers for job retraining and compensatory education are viewed by this group as the best solution to the efficiency and equity problems of providing true educational advancement to the disadvantaged. The poor showing of these educational programs on benefit-cost analysis criteria has been, then, one stimulant pushing educational policy in the direction of social experimentation and perhaps, decentralization.

Rate-of-Return Analysis

There are two main methods used to compare the costs and benefits of alternative investments. One method is to calculate the present values of the costs and the benefits of the investment, and then to take the difference or form a quotient. The streams of costs and benefits have to be discounted by the interest rate to put the future dollars on an equal footing. A major problem with benefit-cost analysis is that the results are very sensitive to the discount rate used, and there is no single discount rate agreed upon by economists. The second method, that of calculating the internal rate of return, skirts this problem. Here, the two present values of costs and benefits are made equal by solving for the discount rate which equates the two figures.

A diagrammatical exposition might make the procedure clearer. Presented in Figure 2-1 are the lifetime earnings streams of two individuals, similar in all respects except that individual II has had one more year of schooling than individual I. Individual I's lifetime earnings stream would be $OAHI$, and individual II's lifetime earnings stream is $DFGI$, which should be compared with the direct costs of tuition and books ($ODCB$), and the foregone earnings ($OAED$).

The internal rate of return of the investment in education can be calculated most easily by finding the discount rate that equates the present value of the increment in earnings (*FEHG*), with the present value of the cost of education (*AECB*). If the internal rate of return is positive, the investment is profitable. This rate of return, however, should be compared to the rates of return on alternative investments, physical and human, before a decision is made to invest or not.

The viability of this procedure for making actual policy decisions depends, of course, upon the quality and validity of the cost and earnings estimates. Some of the difficulties pertaining to the intrinsic nature of human capital have been mentioned already, but a few problems peculiar to educational investment should be examined for possible biases in the rates-of-return analysis.

In calculating the cost side of rate-of-return analysis, the estimate of the direct costs, is perhaps, the most reliable. However, it is problematical whether the costs are private or social. It is the private costs that influence the individual student to invest in a further year of education or not, but it is the cost to society that is important to the policymaker. For primary and secondary schools, the private direct costs are minor, consisting of books, supplies, and perhaps some additional clothing expenses. The social costs include all the private costs plus the direct costs of financing the buildings and paying teachers' salaries and administrative costs. For secondary school students, in particular, it is the opportunity costs of foregone earnings that are the main private costs of education. Because there are two types of costs, private and social, one can see that there must be two types of rates of return, the private or internal rate of return and the social rate of return. There are differences on the benefits side also.

The opportunity costs are the most important cost for the individual, rising with the number of years of education completed. Opportunity costs are also social costs because society foregoes their output. These costs are estimated by comparing similar individuals, one in school and one at work.

A peculiar characteristic of investment in education is that there is thought to be an important consumption element to educational expenditures. There are two components of this consumption element, obtaining the education (the enjoyment of schooling), and the increase in psychic income that education gives one in later life. If these two items are important, they should be subtracted from costs and added to the benefits of education, respectively. Ignoring them produces a downward bias in rate-of-return analysis. As pointed out above, there may be some disutility associated with the educational process and some disutility associated with work later on in life. These factors tend to offset the consumption aspects of education. The following is how one well-known British writer concludes discussion of the dilemma:

It would seem that at this stage, we simply do not know whether to add or to subtract the consumption-benefits from the investment-benefits of education. This is not to say that we can never find out. . . . For the time being, however, the consumption hypothesis may be ruled out by Occam's Razor.[41]

Rate-of-Return Studies

The above qualifications and possible biases should be kept in mind when one examines the empirical evidence on rates-of-return analysis. The first major attempt at estimating the rate of return to education was made by Gary Becker.[42] For white males, Becker calculated an internal rate of return to college graduation of 14.5 percent in 1939, and 13 percent in 1949. Becker is much less sure about the social rate of return, but he sets a lower and upper band of 13 percent and 25 percent to the white-male 1939 cohort.[43] Becker calculated a significantly higher internal rate of return to high school graduates, 28 percent in 1958. Becker's full results are tabulated in Table 3-5.

The return to private physical capital in the United States economy has been estimated at between 10 percent and 15 percent.[44] This is after the deduction of corporate income tax, but before personal income tax. The evidence indicates that investment, especially through the high school years, compares favorably with investment in physical capital. It is also important to note the significant uptrend in the return to high school.

Several other independently derived estimates of college and high school should be mentioned because they use different techniques, data sources and years. According to Schultz, Giora Hanoch has the best earnings profiles now available.[45] Hanoch, using 1960

Table 3-5
Private Rates of Return from College and High School Education for Selected Years since 1939 (Percentage)

Year of Cohort	College Graduates (1)	High School Graduates (2)
1939	14.5	16
1949	13+	20
1956	12.4	25
1958	14.8	28
1959	(Slightly Higher than in 1958)	
1961		

Source: Gary S. Becker, *"Human Capital: A Theoretical and Empirical Analysis, with Special Reference to Education."* © 1964 by the National Bureau of Economic Research (New York: Columbia University Press), p. 128.

census data, calculated rates of return of 18 percent to high school, and 10 percent to college, which he reduces to 16 percent and 9.6 percent, respectively, when adjusted for ability and demographic variables.[46]

W. Lee Hansen, using 1949 data, estimated rates of return of 15.3 percent and 11.6 percent for high school and college, respectively.[47] Differing from the above estimates in using a longitudinal case study method, Daniel Rogers presents slightly conflicting estimates.[48] Rogers feels that his longitudinal method, which is a follow-up study on 1,827 males who took intelligence tests in the eighth and ninth grade in eight high schools in Massachusetts and Connecticut in 1935, is far superior to the usual cross-section method. He is also able to control for many more ability, character, and demographic variables than previous studies. One problem with his study is that he may have a biased sample, because the sample includes mainly prep schools and academic high schools, which are in only one area of the country. Rogers' results are reproduced in Table 3-6.

Rogers' main conclusions are that: "Expenditure on education appears to be a viable investment for all levels through college graduation," and "that education pays off for all people about equally well, regardless of intelligence (at least within wide limits)."[49]

Finally, there is a very recent study by Thomas Johnson which uses Hanoch's data but uses a model of investment behavior that assures that the individual is making continuous decisions as opposed to Becker's discrete model of income generation.[50] Further,

Table 3-6

Estimates of Internal Rates of Return to Investment in Education

	Rogers[a]	
	Unadjusted	Adjusted
From Grade 8 to Grade 12	9.13[a]	6.7[a]
From Grade 12 to 4 Years College	14.15	8.9

[a]Private rates of return before tax for white males. In each cell, the first figure is for high-cost and second for low-cost education.

Source: Daniel C. Rogers, "Private Rates of Return to Education in the United States: A Case Study," *Yale Economic Essays*, 9, no. 1 (Spring 1969): 124.

Johnson's model uses nonlinear estimating techniques and accounts for the depreciation of human capital and the autonomous growth in earnings over time. For white males in the North, the calculated rates of return were 21 percent and 16 percent to high school and college, respectively, generally higher than previous estimates, including Hanoch's.[51]

The major conclusion from all these studies is that at least for white males, high school graduation is definitely a good investment, while a college degree is certainly competitive with alternative physical capital investments. When one considers that the evidence indicates that the social rate of return is likely to be higher than the private rate of return, especially for high school, these conclusions are reinforced. It should be noted that most studies have at the same time shown much lower rates of return to graduate education. The rates are low enough in some cases to call into question the desirability of expanding the graduate educational investment. Hunt and Rogers independently estimate the private rate of return to a second degree from zero to 6 percent, while Johnson's estimate is 10 percent.[52]

A study by Ashenfelter and Mooney, using a follow-up questionnaire on Woodrow Wilson Fellows, provides estimates of rates of return to different types of Ph.D's in the range of 5 percent to 11 percent.[53] Of course, their sample probably biased the rates upward. In contrast to these estimates, Schultz calculated rates of return to graduate education at about 15 percent, although he counted graduate stipends as earnings (for which practice he attempts to make a case).[54] The conclusion with regard to graduate study must be that any more than the current level of investment in graduate education is questionable. Because the social rate of return is not likely to be higher than the private rate and may even be lower due to the states' paying a larger share of the costs, including some of the student's opportunity costs, and, due to the fact that externalities are probably less important, the conclusions, based on the private rate-of-return analysis, are reinforced.

The pattern of rates of return falling with higher levels of education continues at the junior high and elementary level. Schultz and Hanoch's estimates for the return to elementary school range from 35 percent to 100 percent, while Johnson's estimate for the return to junior high school is in the 20 percent to 25 percent range.[55] And again, the biases discussed in the early part of the paper indicate that the social return is apt to be much higher.

The estimates of returns to education range from a high of 100 percent for elementary school to a low of zero for some types of graduate education, and the pattern of a falling rate of return appears to hold at each level of additional schooling. The implications for policymakers are that relatively more funds should be devoted to the lower levels of schooling than are now being allocated.

The Return to Increased Quality

There is specific rate of return evidence on the effects of increasing the quality of education. Quality of schooling can be increased by paying higher salaries and hiring better teachers or improving the physical plant. One estimate of the return to paying teachers (elementary and high school) higher salaries in rural and farm areas made by Welch is between 23 percent and 26 percent.[56] Many studies have also examined the link between the quality of school inputs and the output of schooling as measured by verbal achievement scores. This is the problem of estimating the so-called educational production function.[57] Because these studies do not estimate the returns to improved quality of inputs, they cannot be used to determine the amount of resources that should be allocated to education in general or among different levels of education. Once rate-of-return analysis has established that more funds should be allocated to a given type of educational investment project, the educational production functions studies can be used to determine how the funds should be allocated among the various inputs. Rate-of-return analysis can be fairly easily combined with production function studies once the link between higher verbal scores and earnings is estimated.

Because estimating educational production functions is in its infancy, most studies stop with verbal scores as a measure of output. Here is another area where further work needs to be done. H. M. Levin, in writing a summary of the literature in this area, concluded that the one clear finding that stood out in almost all the studies of this type was that teacher salary levels and student achievement showed a positive and statistically significant relationship when other measurable influences were held constant.[58] The assumption, of course, is that higher teacher salaries mean better teachers. Levin himself has found that obtaining teachers with higher verbal scores is five to ten times more effective per dollar in raising student verbal scores than obtaining teachers with more experience.[59]

4

Educational Investment and Discrimination

Discrimination and Rate-of-Return Analysis

One area where rate-of-return analysis has given economists insights is the problem of discrimination. Rate-of-return studies for blacks and whites have been attempted by many economists. Gary Becker estimated the rate of return to the 1939 cohort of urban, nonwhite male college graduates to be about 12.3 percent in the South and 8.3 percent in the North.[1] This compares with the 14.5 percent return that Becker found for United States, white urban males. The returns are lower for nonwhites, even though the costs of attending black colleges were estimated by Becker to be lower than the costs of white colleges. The lower rates of return to education for blacks are due, then, to their lower earnings relative to whites. For example, in 1939, the nonwhite to white mean wage and salary income ratio for urban males age fifteen to sixty-five was 40.5 percent in the South and 58.2 percent in the North and West.[2] In 1967, the ratio of black to white mean incomes for all males over twenty-four years old was 57.4 percent.[3]

Most of this rather large disparity can be ascribed to discrimination. Past discrimination has denied the blacks equal educational, job, health, housing, and social opportunities, all of which have affected the earning potential of blacks. A broad enough conception of discrimination could, of course, explain all of the difference since even some of the heredity differences that may or may not affect earning capacities are probably due to the 400 years of slavery and discrimination suffered by the black race in North America. The point for public policymakers is, of course, that society is morally obligated to correct this situation in as short a time as possible. Because educational achievement is the major determinant of both earning capacity and the income differences between blacks and whites,[a] this chapter will examine the relationships between educa-

---

[a]J. Gwartney estimates that about five-eighths of the income differential between whites and nonwhites is due to differences in educational attainment and achievement with the rest being

tion and discrimination with the dual intent of determining measures to correct the earnings gap and of estimating the payoff of public policy actions that do attempt to close the gap.

Theories of Discrimination

Before we get into the discussion of how a lack of education and a tendency to discriminate interact and reinforce each other, a theory of discrimination around which to organize our thought is needed. There are several theories of discrimination. Social psychologists maintain that discrimination which is the active component of ethnic prejudice is "an antipathy based upon a faulty and inflexible generalization, . . ." the net effect of which is "to place the object of prejudice at some disadvantage not merited by his own misconduct."[4] In other words, discrimination has its basis in ignorance. The policy implication of this definition, which psychologists as a whole have not been afraid to spell out and call for, is that educational programs ranging from presenting facts to role playing should be used to eliminate such asocial behavior.

Not all psychologists agree, however, with the above definition, but argue instead that attitudes are prejudiced only if they violate the important norms or values accepted in a culture.[5] In other words, as long as the majority holds a certain attitude or reacts against another group in a certain way, there can be nothing morally reprehensible about such behavior. By this reasoning, South African Apartheid, the nineteenth century Indian caste system, or eighteenth century United States slavery were not examples of prejudicial or discriminatory behavior. Unfortunately, the mainstream of economic thought held until recently an even more conservative approach to the problems posed by discrimination. Milton Friedman states: "It is hard to see that discrimination can have any meaning other than a 'taste' of others that one does not share."[6] Friedman goes on to say that "distaste" for blacks is fundamentally no different from a "taste" for pretty girls. This definition is quite similar to the above relativistic definition held by some psychologists except that now any "taste," even if it is abnormal or outside the group norm, must

explained by the differences in other demographic features and job discrimination. See J. Gwartney, "Discrimination and Income Differentials," *The American Economic Review* 60 (June 1970): 412.

BOOK ORDER FORM

HOLD
CODE

ALPHA
PREFIX

CL. NO.			
ACC. NO.			
DLR NO.	M L S		
ORD NO.	3/6669		
LIST	10.50 COST		
DATE ORD	2-11-74	FUND Sec.Ed.	
DATE REC		REV. BY Haynes	

AUTH Davis, J. Ronnie & Morrall, J.F.

TITLE EVALUATING EDUCATIONAL INVESTMENT

PLACE

YR 1973

COPIES 1

VOLS

PUBL Lexington

SBN

SERIES
EDITION

SUBSCRIBER NAME

VAR. IN EDITION   F

NO. OF COPIES OF CARDS WANTED

NYP July. 4-8-74
NYP " 8/6/74

D262

be accepted by the social scientist. To "scientific" or "positivistic" economists, taste must be considered one of the "givens."

The public policy implications of this type of framework are, of course, that there should be no public policy in this area. All is not lost, however, because Friedman maintains that because discrimination is inefficient, it will be eliminated by competition.[7] Friedman's optimism was based on the conclusion of the only rigorous theoretical and empirical investigation into the phenomenon of discrimination by an economist that existed at that time. This pioneering investigation, *The Economics of Discrimination*,[8] was completed by Milton Friedman's most famous student, Gary Becker.

Becker assumes from the start that discrimination is just another "taste" for which an individual would be willing to pay a sum of money for satisfaction.[9] From the start, Becker rejects the socio-psychological definition of discrimination because he feels that "it is not necessary to get involved in these more philosophical issues."[10] But in so doing, Becker predetermines the outcome of his model and the public policy implications of it. Since whites must pay a price for discrimination, whites as well as blacks are hurt in monetary terms relative to a situation where whites have no taste for discrimination. But given a taste for discrimination, whites maximize their utility by discriminating. Thus those members of society who have no taste for discrimination will have a competitive edge over their more prejudiced rivals. In the long run, given a distribution of differences in tastes for discrimination, it will be eliminated by the market place and the law of survival of the fittest. There seems to be something lacking in a theory in which discrimination is not stable in the long run. There must, therefore, be something more to discrimination than just tastes, as Friedman and Becker would have us believe, or even ignorance, as Allport maintains.

It seems incongrous that Becker's basic model would be extremely well adapted to focus on the basic economic rationale for discrimination. Keeping the model, but changing its basic assumption—that discrimination is a "taste"—results in a much more plausible set of conclusions and important positive public policy implications. Becker's model also can be used to explore the "discrimination is ignorance thesis." It will be worthwhile to develop Becker's model of discrimination despite the fact that it is based upon the rather complicated Heckscher-Ohlin model of international trade.[11] But first, the third basis of discrimination must be presented.

It is clear that the persistence and permeation of discrimination in all major societies must serve a functional purpose. Here again, psychologists have led economists in explaining the implications of this possibility by maintaining that prejudice can serve many purposes including outlets for the pathological personality, the economically frustrated, and the self-defensive or "ego-defenders."[12] The emphasis on the part of psychologists on economic frustration, and the need to feel superior as the basis of the functional nature of discrimination, should emphasize to economists, with their broader perspective, the basic economic determinist nature of discrimination.[b] The majority enforces discrimination on the minority most likely because it is profitable to do so. While social psychologists do downplay the profit motive and talk instead about social status and self-defense, economists cannot.[c]

Becker's Model

As pointed out above, Becker's model, although quite unintentionally, does bring this point home most closely. Becker hypothesizes a world of whites and blacks who do not trade with each other in products but who may exchange the factors of production, labor, and capital.[13] Becker further assumes that whites are capital abundant relative to blacks, that blacks are labor abundant relative to whites, that whites have a preference to exchange labor and capital with whites rather than blacks, and that whites are in fact willing to pay a premium for this privilege. It should be remembered that even in 1957, Becker meant that concept "capital" to include human as

---

[b]It is mildly surprising that the Chicago school of economics, which has pioneered in applying classical microeconomics and its cornerstone of profit maximization in analyses on social and political phenomenon, should have lagged behind other social scientists and economists in recognizing this important facet of discrimination.

[c]A popular paperback frequently used in principles of economics courses fails even to mention the economic motivating facet of discrimination. See D. North and R. Miller, *The Economics of Public Issues* (New York: Harper & Row Publishers, 1971), pp. 136-37. Perhaps this is in reaction to the Marxian interpretation of discrimination which attributes racial prejudice to the need on the part of whites "to rationalize and justify the robbery, enslavement, and continued exploitation of their colored victims all over the globe," and which has been discredited by most mainstream economists. See, P. Boran and P. Sweezy, "Monopoly, Capitalism and Race Relations," *Up Against the American Myth*, T. Christoffel et al., eds. (New York: Holt Paperback, 1970), pp. 277-90.

well as physical capital. However, recent developments in international economics have emphasized the importance of human over physical capital in explaining trade patterns.[14] And indeed, in a model of discrimination where the identity of the owner of capital is crucial, human capital should be doubly important. Physical capital is too homogeneous and fungible to be an effective agent of discrimination.

As demonstrated in trade theory, a free-trade situation—that is, no discrimination—is superior for both groups (in the sense that both groups are able to consume a larger bundle of goods) than in the autarky case, that is, complete discrimination or segregation.[15] According to Becker, intermediate degrees of discrimination harm both races according to the intensity of the discrimination or "tariff."[16] Becker also points out that given similar demand conditions between blacks and whites, well-balanced production functions, and several other generally made assumptions in theoretical economics, whites will "export" their relative cheap factor, capital, to blacks, while blacks will "export" their relatively inexpensive factor, labor. According to the Stolper-Samuelson theorem, furthermore, trade will increase the return to society's abundant factor of production and reduce the return to the scarce factor.[17] White laborers and black capitalists will thus be in favor of discrimination, while white capitalists and black laborers will be in favor of free trade, that is, the elimination of discrimination. According to Becker, however, this is not something that can or should be eliminated by public policy.

Becker points out that these results are in direct opposition to the Marxian interpretation of discrimination—that is, that capitalists promote prejudice in order to stigmatize and more easily exploit a given group.[18] Note, however, that this point is only true if the group discriminated against is abundant in unskilled labor and thus the Marxian and trade model explanations are not in conflict when the discrimination is against a minority abundant in skilled labor such as may have been in the case with the discrimination Marx was more familiar with, discrimination against the Jews. The rigorous theoretical analysis of which groups gain and which lose from discrimination is probably Becker's most important contribution to the theory of discrimination. His theory explains the findings of social psychologists that low-income groups and the economically frustrated are the most highly prejudiced against blacks[19] while white anti-Semitism has frequently been found to be most intense at the country club.

Unfortunately, Becker did not push the trade analogy far enough. Anne Krueger has pointed out that Becker neglected the terms of trade effect of tariffs or, in this case, the terms of trade effects of discrimination.[20] Krueger shows that even if whites have no "tastes" for discrimination, whites would still discriminate if they wished to maximize their incomes. The theory of optimum tariffs, or discrimination, shows that as long as the foreign offer curve is not perfectly elastic, whites can always gain by discrimination and moreover, that there is an optimum degree of discrimination that maximizes white incomes.[21] Krueger also points out that another way that the majority group could distort the allocation of capital and exploit the minority is to deny public educational investment to the minority through the mechanism of the ballot box.[22] This method also would decrease society's income in comparison with the no discrimination case, but it would give whites a larger piece of the smaller pie.

A Trade Theory of Discrimination

In international trade theory, it can usually be shown that the second country can in turn impose an "optimum" tariff and recoup some of its losses, but again, at the expense of the other country. This recognition of the possibilities of retaliation and tariff wars is usually thought to lead rational governments to mutual tariff reductions, especially since one country is usually not large relative to the rest of the world.[d] But the situation of the blacks in the United States, according to this framework, is rather hopeless. Since blacks are outnumbered in physical terms by about 9 to 1, and in economic power by about 20 to 1, they are a relatively small "country." In terms of offer curves, the black community is probably facing an almost perfectly elastic white offer curve while their own offer curve is relatively inelastic. This means that they cannot influence the terms of trade established by the white community. This possibility is shown in Figure 4-1. The white free-trade offer curve, OW, shows the various amounts of capital that whites are willing and able to exchange for given amounts of black labor, while the black offer curve, OB, shows the amounts of labor that blacks would be willing

---

[d]When one country is large relative to other countries, frequently charges of "exploitation" and imperialism are raised here also.

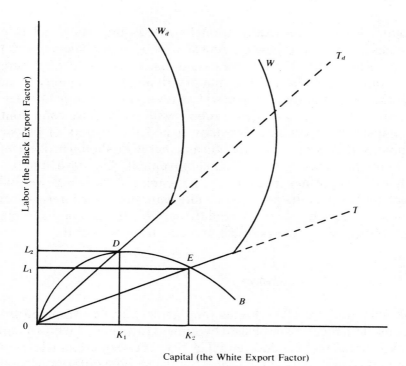

Figure 4-1. White-black Offer Curves and the Terms of Trade

and able to exchange for given amounts of white capital. At the point where the two offers coincide, at point E, equilibrium will be established and the terms of trade will be OT. Now note that if whites discriminate against black labor by reducing their offer to OW_d, the white community can shift the terms of trade OT_d against the blacks receiving L_1L_2 more black labor for K_1K_2 less white capital. Since the terms of trade, OT_d and OW_d, correspond at point D, the black community cannot discriminate against white capital and hope to improve their terms of trade. Indeed, if they do, their situation will surely worsen because the volume of trade will be reduced with no corresponding improvement in their terms of trade.

If the economic or exploitation factor is important in the discrimination against the blacks in the United States, discrimination will be harder to reduce than if it were due to just ignorance or "tastes." Ignorance can be eliminated by education, and competition should reduce discrimination of the "taste" variety, and in both cases, the elimination of discrimination improves the welfare of both groups. Even if the exploitation motive is important, all is not hopeless. There are several reasons to be optimistic on strictly economic grounds. First, to the extent that a more equal distribution of income is a public good or that discrimination is a public "bad" the white community would be willing to sacrifice income in order to purchase these commodities. Second, within the white community, capitalists, both educated manpower and the owners of physical capital, suffer from discrimination and therefore should prove useful allies of blacks in the integrationist movement. And third, and probably most important, because the per capita black losses would be much higher than the per capita white gain, the black interest group should be more highly motivated to work for the end of discrimination, either within the political process or outside of it.

The Cost of Discrimination

The magnitude of these losses (and gains) can be estimated from income data recently published by James Gwartney,[23] who attempts to explain the income differential in 1959 between urban whites and nonwhites (males) by estimating what the income differential would be if nonwhites had the same quantity of education in terms of years, the same scholastic achievement as measured in the Coleman Report, and the same state, rural-urban, and age distribution as the white population. He found that the unadjusted nonwhite to white income ratio rose from about 58 percent to 84 percent, leaving 16 percent unexplained, presumably by employment discrimination.[24] In terms of 1960 national income, this amounts to about $7.125 billion.[25]

As argued above, this is not the only source of economic discrimination since the quality and quantity of education received by blacks has certainly been lower due, at least in part, to the knowledge upon the part of blacks that they faced low rates of return and job discrimination after graduation. In addition, discrimination in past public educational investment funding has certainly reduced the earnings potential of blacks. The loss due to the lower quantity and quality of education adds about $4.5 billion and $7.125 billion, respectively, to the above figure, bringing the total to $18.75 billion.[26] In terms of 1970 GNP, the total loss would have doubled to about $37.5 billion, assuming there has been no significant progress in fighting the economic manifestations of discrimination.[27] This amounts to about $1,900 per black per year, but only about $140 per white. If the distributional gain for whites is roughly equal to the efficiency loss of the society due to discrimination (which appears likely because of theoretical considerations and previous empirical work),[28] then the $37.5 billion can be considered a deadweight loss to society. The costs of providing increased quantity and quality of education to blacks should, of course, be subtracted from this estimate, but given the new phenomenon of unemployed teachers and unused physical capacity, the social costs of employing teachers would be quite small, and therefore the gross social gains of $37.5 billion probably only slightly overstate the net social gain.[e]

Educational Investment and Discrimination

The magnitude of this gain, especially on a per capita basis for blacks, indicates that public policy aimed at eliminating this loss would produce high economic, as well as social, returns. In order to analyze the public policy implications in this area, especially as they apply to education, a construct relating blacks to whites to education and discrimination must be developed, and the various types of discrimination discussed above incorporated into it. Figure 4-2 shows some of the ways that discrimination and education are related to each other. Arrows I and IV show the effect of increasing the quantity-quality nexus of education of whites and blacks, respectively, on the degree of discrimination of whites against blacks; while arrows III and II show the effect of reducing discrimination on whites and blacks' attitudes, respectively, toward education.

In case I, an increase in investment in white education should reduce the overall degree of discrimination of whites against blacks irrespective of whether the discrimination is based on ignorance, "tastes," or exploitation. If education reduces the misconceptions and misinformation that whites have about blacks and their inflexibility and prejudice in general, it is not hard to see how discrimina-

---

[e]Actually, since the income figures used are for urban whites and nonwhites and since the rural figures show a greater differential, the gross estimate is biased downward. Also, it would be more revealing if this estimate were put in rate of return form which could be done if the actual social cost of educating the blacks were available, since the $37.5 billion represents a yearly flow.

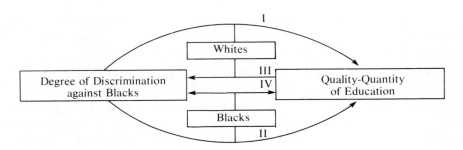

Figure 4-2. The Nexus of Discrimination and Education

tion would be reduced.[f] Second, if, as seems likely, discrimination is similar to a "demerit" want,[g] then once whites have been educated, their "tastes" for discrimination are likely to decline. And, finally, according to the exploitation theory, since white capitalists, including human capitalists, suffer declines in income due to discrimination, as more whites accumulate human capital, it is in their economic interest to work or "trade" with unskilled black labor.

Unfortunately, the results are not as clear in case II as in case I. In case II, the question is how does an increase in black human capital affect the degree of discrimination to which blacks themselves are subjected? As blacks gain more education and therefore, on that account alone, become more like whites, white discrimination based on ignorance and tastes should decline. But offsetting this tendency is the implication of the "economic" model of discrimination that the presently existing black capitalists will suffer relative declines in real income with movements toward reduced discrimination. According to this theory, it is in the interests of black skilled labor to provoke whites into discriminating against blacks in general. Although some black skilled labor, such as teachers, lawyers and physicians, might be hurt by integration in the short run, clearly,

---

[f]Actually, it might not be that easy to see when it is recalled that social psychologists view prejudice as attitudes which are clung to even when one is confronted with facts that contradict previously held views. However, to the extent that the new information is in dissonance with the old beliefs and one identifies with other educated individuals, the theory of cognitive dissonance predicts that prejudice should be reduced. See L. Festinger, *A Theory of Cognitive Dissonance* (Evanston, Ill.: Row, Peterson, 1957).

[g]Musgrave defines *merit wants* as goods or services that are not purchased in the private market by consumers (but could be) because they are uninformed as to the true nature of the commodity. Once informed, their preference patterns are modified in such a way that they would purchase the good. Discrimination may be the obverse of such a good. See R. Musgrave, *The Theory of Public Finance* (New York: McGraw-Hill Book Company, 1959), pp. 13-14.

in the long run, the black community as a whole would be better off through increased "trade" with the white community, and therefore the leaders of the black community are likely to share in the increase in income also. This phenomenon, however, might explain some of the motivating force for the black separatists' movement.

Cases III and IV involve the effect of a reduction in discrimination on the supply and demand, respectively, of black human capital. Presumably a decline in the white propensity to discriminate against blacks, for whatever reason it occurs, would mean that whites would be more willing to provide a greater quality and quantity of educational investment to the black community. At the very least, in a world of no discrimination, by definition whites would be willing to provide equal educational opportunity to blacks.[h] According to Finis Welch, however, the major gains to blacks should come from the demand side. Given job discrimination and the prospects of lower salaries than whites after graduation, the decision of many blacks to spend less time and effort in school is actually a rational one. Welch has estimated that over 50 percent of the white to nonwhite income differential observed between rural southern male high school graduates in 1955 was due to market discrimination against education while only 30 percent was due to the inferior quality of schooling received by blacks, with the rest of the difference attributed to market discrimination against physical labor.[29] Equal job opportunities would thus call forth from blacks greater investment of money, time and effort in human capital.

The complex four-way interrelationships between discrimination and investment in education point out that the relationship between black educational investment, discrimination and earnings are not apt to be a simple additive function.[30] Indeed, the preceding

---

[h]That black schools were separate but equal before 1954, of course, is a myth which Welch has dispelled with the following data for 1955:

	Total Current Expenditure Per Pupil	Mem. of Instructional Staff per 100 Pupils	Average Salary per Member of Instructional Staff	Average No. of Pupils Enrolled Per Secondary School
White	$230	4.6	$3,330	230
Nonwhite	120	4.0	2,310	175

See F. Welch, "Labor-Market Discrimination: An Interpretation of Income Differences in the Rural South," *The Journal of Political Economy* 75 (June 1967): 237.

argument has shown that black educational investment and discrimination are complementary factors in determining the returns to human capital. Therefore most rate-of-return analysis, such as Becker's, which shows the effect on earnings of increasing the years spent in formal education while holding all other factors constant, seriously underestimates the returns to education because, as argued above, increased education should reduce discrimination. This also means that rate-of-return analysis or cost-benefit analysis of programs aimed at the reduction of job discrimination that do not take into account the repercussions of educational investment will be seriously underestimated.

The most recent rate-of-return estimates to investment in education, those of Thomas Johnson, are strongly biased downward, especially for blacks. For example, the return to an eighth grade education for southern whites is 19.6 percent and for southern nonwhites, 18.1 percent, while the returns to high school are 22.3 percent and 22.0 percent, to college, 17.3 percent and 13.5 percent, and to graduate school, 9.3 percent and 5.0 percent for whites and blacks, respectively.[31] The private rate of returns as well as the social rates of return to investment in black education are thus seriously underestimated if the complementary interrelationships between discrimination and education are as important as is argued above. The policy conclusions from this analysis are that investment in the education of blacks and legal and educational campaigns against discrimination should be pursued in consonance and with force.

Finally, recent empirical studies by Randall Weiss came to even stronger conclusions.[32] Based on a recursive regression model that attempted to determine the relationship between education and earnings for blacks and whites, Weiss concluded: "Given a labor market that distributed rewards among blacks without regard to their education, the solution to the black poverty problem seems to be outside this classroom."[33]

This conclusion certainly is too pessimistic with regard to education because Weiss's model, although it did take into account the effect of discrimination on the returns to education, failed to take into account the reverse effect that education should have on discrimination. Only when models taking into account the full complementarities of education and discrimination are specified and estimated can correct statements about the returns to the education of blacks and whites be made.

5 Educational Investment and Economic Growth

Factors in Economic Growth

To this point, we have concentrated mainly on the allocation and distributional aspects of educational investment. We now turn to another way of evaluating educational investment. How does education influence the size of a nation's output?

Economic growth may be regarded as increasing total national product or as raising future output, although any reasonable concern for economic growth must be for increasing per capita real income over time.[a] Increasing national product requires either (1) some addition in the quantity of productive resources, (2) some improvement in the quality of given resources, or (3) some more effective method of utilizing given resources. Since land is assumed to be fixed in quantity, this means that increases in total national product may be due to the use of more or better labor, the use of more or better physical capital, or more efficient use of labor, materials and machines.

The Quantity of Productive Resources

The use of more labor may contribute to an increase in per capita national product only if the ratio of working to nonworking people increases.[b] This ratio depends in turn on many factors, such as the

---

[a]As all know who have choked on air fouled by increased production, there are serious weaknesses in the popular presumption that a rise in per capita real income is a "good thing" in itself. The problem is that no provision is made for "negative goods" or "bads" in the commonly employed indices of measurement. For a widely acclaimed discussion of the costs of economic growth, see E. J. Mishan, *The Costs of Economic Growth* (London: Staples Press, 1967) and *Technology and Growth* (New York: Praeger, 1970). For attempts to design indices which capture the positive and negative "signs"—that is, the pluses and minuses of economic and social change—see *Toward a Social Report* (Washington: U.S. Department of HEW, 1969).

[b]Population increases have been emphasized in the discussion of economic growth and development since the eighteenth century. Adam Smith, generally regarded as the progenitor

age composition of the population, the labor-force participation rate, the employment rate, and the length of the workweek. Education may influence (either positively or negatively) all of these factors, particularly the labor-force participation rate.

In a study of the census weeks of 1940, 1950, and 1960, Bowen and Finegan recently showed that education is associated positively with the U.S. participation rate.[1] In Table 5-1, the 1960 labor-force participation rates for males between the ages of thirty-five and forty-four are shown to increase from 67.2 percent for those with no schooling completed to 98.7 with sixteen years completed. For less than twelve years of schooling completed, the labor participation rates are shown to decline between 1940 and 1960. Two important factors may explain this trend: (1) the increased industrial recognition of certification norms, and (2) the effective expansion of compulsory schooling.

The reason seems evident for the strong, positive relationship between education and the labor-force participation rate. By staying out of the labor force, the more educated person has more to lose economically than a less educated person. Generalizations can be hazardous, however. In predominantly agricultural countries, for example, participation in the labor force may often be associated negatively with education. In short, an educated person may refuse to do agricultural work because he is "above" working as a common laborer, but he cannot be absorbed elsewhere in an economy which does not provide any alternative job opportunities.[2] "Overeducated" unemployment may also occur in highly industrialized societies which have produced too many Ph.D.'s, for example.

Basically, the use of more physical capital depends on the saving and investment decisions of an economy. Bringing about an increase in the quantity of physical capital calls for the diversion of current

---

of modern economics, was optimistic that a growing population made possible an increasing division and specialization of labor. As the labor force expanded, each worker could become more and more a specialist by concentrating on or mastering a few skills or even one, and by that means, foster increased productivity. Smith's unbounded optimism was countered by the pessimism of Thomas Robert Malthus and David Ricardo, both of whom regarded population growth an anathema leading to absolute declines in per capita income to the point where no economic progress could take place. In their theories, population made unrealized demands on food supply so that there would be recurring waves of endemic starvation and misery. The only class accumulating wealth would be landowners who, as wastrels, were not likely to invest in real capital formation. And capital investment was one of only a few ways to avoid the specter of the "stationary state," which was a condition of such utter despair that it earned for economics its renown as the "dismal science."

Table 5-1

Schooling and Labor Force Participation: Males 35-44, Census Weeks of 1940, 1950, 1960

Males 35-44 by Years of School Completed	Labor Force Participation Rate		
	1940[a]	1950	1960
0	77.7	80.5	67.5
1-4	91.3	91.9	87.1
5-7	93.4[b]	93.8	91.4
8	95.4[b]	95.6	94.4
9-11	96.1	96.2	95.9
12	96.3	97.0	97.7
13-15	96.2	96.6	97.7
16	97.3[c]	97.7[c]	98.7
17+			98.6
Total	94.8	94.6	95.6

[a]The participation rates in the 1940 column are for native-born whites only.

[b]In 1940, data was reported for 5-6 and 7-8 years of school completed.

[c]The 1940 and 1950 reports did not give separate labor-free estimates for persons with 17+ years of school completed.

Source: William G. Bowen and T. Aldrich Finegan, "The Economics of Labor Force Participation." © 1969 by Princeton University Press, Table 3-6, p. 60. Reprinted by permission.

resources away from consumption now and consumption in the future. As such, these decisions would be made on the basis of comparisons between individuals' (time) preference for present versus future goods and the productivity of the investment in raising future output. By aggregating all such individual decisions, the growth rate of the economy is determined. This process is referred to as the competitive determination of an economy's growth path.

This "classical" microeconomic version of economic growth focuses, therefore, on bringing about an increase in physical capital and discovering more effective ways of using given resources. Two serious challenges have been levied at this version. The first challenge to competitive determination of economic growth came initially out of the work of John Maynard Keynes and others.[8] Particularly on the basis of work by Harrod and Domar, the nature of this challenge was that, because of the unemployment of resources, the aggregation of individual decisions may lead to a growth rate which is unsatisfactory.[4]

The second challenge to competitive determination of the growth rate grew out of the "externalities" discussion. Not all of the benefits or costs of some growth-related activities may accrue to the individual(s) concerned. Accordingly, the decision would be based on incomplete social data, which is to say that social evaluation of costs and benefits might result in either more or less economic growth. In the 1930s, the argument was that private decisions result in too little growth because of defective "telescopic" faculty.[5] In the 1970s, however, there is increasing consensus that private decisions may result in too much growth.[6]

In any event, although education may influence both saving and investment decisions, the influence may be either positive or negative. Even so, the influence is likely to be too slight and indirect and slow to be taken into account in educational planning.

The Quality of Productive Resources

In the 1950s, evidence began to accumulate that quantity changes in labor and capital were by no means as dominant or even as significant as had been thought earlier by most economists.[7] There was a large "residual" of growth that could not be explained statistically in terms of the usual inputs. Eventually, it became clear that the residual was greater as the growth rate was larger—that is, the conventional models worked well only when there was relatively little growth to be explained.[8] Although factors of economic growth other than quantity changes in labor and physical capital had long been recognized, the size of the residual was surprising.[c]

The residual was attributed to technical change, technological progress, or to the increased "productivity" per unit of input employed. (Modern large-scale research is now highly organized and is shifting some of the emphasis to "research and development," which, of course, has many links to education.) It was understood that technological progress (or research and development) had the effect of promoting a change in the quality of capital inputs employed, which in its turn aided in promoting the rate of economic growth.

Education may have some effect on the use of better physical capital. Education may train people who then will have the capacity for research and development. Also, education may serve to make

---

[c]The results led many economists to question the validity of models using the "Cobb-Douglas production function" and of the data to which they were applied. See John Vaizey, *The Economics of Education* (New York: Free Press of Glencoe, 1962), p. 39.

people more capable of using improved machinery as well as more alert to, and interested in, its availability and use.

A logical extension of the idea of a change in the quality of physical capital was to apply it to labor. As a matter of fact, the aforementioned residual of unexplained economic growth once was referred to as the "human factor." Although the literature of the 1950s did not develop exhaustively the possible ways in which education could affect the contribution of labor to output, it was fully recognized that the rate of growth could be increased not only by increasing physical capital, but also by a conscious effort to improve the quality of labor through education. This soon led to attempts to identify and to measure the influence of education on the contribution of labor to economic growth.

Obviously, it is with regard to improvements in the quality of labor that education can make its most direct and significant contribution to economic growth.[d] Machlup lists five positive effects which may be expected: (1) better working habits and efforts, greater discipline and reliability; (2) better health through more wholesome living; (3) improved skills and efficiency, better understanding of work requirements; (4) prompter adaptability to changes; and (5) increased mobility to more productive occupations when opportunities arise.[9] In addition, economic growth may be affected simply by improving the allocation and use of given resources. For example, Denison found for nine countries (including the United States) that they had an excessive allocation of labor to agriculture. National product and national product per employed person was smaller, in other words, than these could have been with a smaller percentage of the labor force allocated to agriculture and a larger proportion to nonfarm production.[10] Most of these ways have little or nothing to do with education.

Mystery of the Econometric Residual

Studies of the sources of, or contributions to, economic growth usually begin by trying to measure the effect on national income of increments in resources and of improvements in their quality and use. The part of an increase in national income that is not "ex-

---

[d]However, many economists have looked more to unmeasured improvements in the quality of physical capital than in the quality of labor. See Bowman, "Education and Economic Growth," pp. 89-90.

plained" statistically by increments in labor and physical capital is called the "residual." In the early literature, the residual was considered simply as technical progress, and the studies ended there. Other studies began to dissect the residual.[11] "Embodiment" models developed by Robert Solow and others tried to separate the part of technical progress that was "embodied" in newer capital from the part "disembodied" in more efficient production processes and more efficient use of resources. [12] Other studies, such as the pioneering one by T. W. Schultz and those of E. F. Denison, tried to disaggregate the contribution of education.

Stock of Education

T. W. Schultz compared real income in 1929 and 1957 and calculated the portion not "explained" statistically by increments of labor and physical capital.[13] He then compared the "total value of the stock of education" in 1957 with that of 1930 and separated the increase in the stock of education into (1) the part invested in the increased labor force necessary to give each worker the average education of 1930, and (2) the part ("stock of education added") invested in raising the educational level of the average worker.

Schultz applied this method to the longer period of 1900 to 1957 and found that the stock of education has risen from $63 billion in 1900 to $535 billion in 1957 (both series measured in 1956 schooling costs).[14] These stocks were equivalent to 22 percent and 42 percent, respectively, of "non-human reproducible wealth" in the same years.[15] Clearly, educational capital could be a significant factor of production, and Schultz's study indicated it was becoming relatively more important. For example, the stock of education in the labor force rose over the period by eight and one-half times, whereas physical assets rose by only four and one-half times.

The most basic idea advanced by Schultz was that investment in education has yielded a return in the form of a faster than otherwise rate of growth of national income. The idea itself has been accepted widely by economists and is not in question at this time. On the other hand, there have been warnings about the numerical results ranging from arguments that empirical evidence is too meager to support the large amount of theorizing,[16] to suggestions that Schultz's estimates should be interpreted with care.[17] Despite misgivings about the methodology and data, however, no serious doubt has been cast on the theory itself, and the concepts developed by Schultz have been accepted as clearly relevant to the analysis of the growth process.

Education and the Level of Output

The next logical and important step in this approach was to measure the contributions that changes in the quality of labor have on the level of output. The most ambitious and comprehensive treatment of this aspect is that of Denison, who attempted to assess the contribution of education to economic growth by using the incomes of the educated as an indicator of the returns to education.[e]

Denison's first study dealt with the period 1909-1957, which he separated into two periods, 1909-1929 and 1929-1957. He estimated the growth rate in real national income to have been 2.82 percent annually during 1909-1929 and 2.93 percent annually for 1929-1957. Denison estimated the sources of this growth as follows: (1) additions to the stock of physical capital were estimated to have accounted for 0.73 and 0.43 percentage points, respectively, for the two periods; (2) changes in the labor force contributed 1.53 and 1.57 percentage points, respectively, made up of both quantity and quality changes; and (3) the major quality change in labor was education, which contributed 0.35 and 0.67 percentage points, respectively. Changes in both capital and labor accounted for growth rates of only 2.26 and 2.00 percent, respectively, however, leaving unexplained sizable residual "productivity" increases of 0.56 percent and 0.93 percent. Even so, Denison estimated that education was a significant source of economic growth, accounting for 12 percent of total growth in the first period and 23 percent in the second period.[f]

[e]See Edward F. Denison, *The Sources of Economic Growth in the United States and the Alternatives Before Us* (New York: Committee for Economic Development, 1962); *Why Growth Rates Differ;* "Measuring the Contribution of Education to Economic Growth," *The Residual Factor and Economic Growth* (Paris: Organization for Economic Cooperation and Development, 1964), pp. 13-55. Denison's technique basically is to feed rates of return to education into a production function of the Cobb-Douglas type. The kinds of results yielded by this approach rest upon many analogies with capital theory, the validity of marginal productivity hypothesis, and the acceptability of his methods of measuring education inputs, all of which have been challenged widely.

[f]For the second period, Denison distributed the residual over a range of other factors, the two most important of which were "advances in knowledge" and economies of scale, accounting for 0.58 percent and 0.35 percent, respectively. If advances in knowledge are considered to be educational in nature, then the relative importance of education is even greater. For a highly

Table 5-2
Sources of Economic Growth in Nine Western Nations 1950-1962 (As Estimated by Edward F. Denison)

| | Growth Rates in Percentage Points per Annum | | | | | | Proportion of Total Growth Explained By: | |
| | Contributions of Factor Inputs | | | | | | | |
	Total Growth (1)	Physical Capital (2)	Employment (3)	Education (4)	Other Labor Adjustments (5)[a]	Increased Output per Unit of Input (6)	Education (7)	Output per Unit of Input (8)
United States	3.36	0.83	0.90	0.49	-0.27	1.41	15	42
Belgium	3.03	0.41	0.40	0.43	-0.07	1.86	14	61
Denmark	3.36	0.96	0.70	0.14	-0.25	1.81	4	54
France	4.70	0.79	0.08	0.29	0.08	3.46	6	74
Germany	7.26	1.41	1.49	0.11	-0.23	4.48	2	62
Netherlands	4.52	1.04	0.78	0.24	-0.15	2.61	5	58
Norway	3.47	0.89	0.13	0.24	-0.22	2.43	7	70
United Kingdom	2.38	0.51	0.50	0.29	-0.19	1.27	12	53
Italy	5.95	0.70	0.42	0.40	0.14	4.29	7	72

[a]Adjustments are for mean hours worked and changes in the age and sex composition of the labor force.

Source: Bowman, "Education and Economic Growth," p. 93, derived in turn from Dension, *Why Growth Rates Differ*, Tables 21-1 through 21-20.

A later study by Denison dealing with the United States and eight Western European countries for the period of 1950-1962 showed sharply different results. In Table 5-2, column 4, it can be seen that only for three countries—United States (0.49), Belgium (0.43), and Italy (0.40)—did education account for as much as 0.4 to 0.5 percentage points in national income growth per annum. And only for three countries—United States (15 percent), Belgium (14 percent), and United Kingdom (12 percent)—did education account for as much as 10 percent of the total growth rate (see column 7). Only 2 percent of Germany's total growth is attributed to education. Again, it is all too apparent that it is easier to "explain little growth than much growth."

Denison's calculations have been highly controversial, and acceptance of them seems based on attitudes toward the validity of his measurement procedures.[18] Objections have been levied at everything from an alleged misapplication of the marginal productivity theory of income[g] to an alleged arbitrariness in allocating increased earnings accounted for by ability and by education.[h] Several observations seem warranted. First, those economists who tend to accept Denison's results as a first approximation (except for detail and misleading claims of accuracy) are generally those who accept the validity of the connection between income shares and marginal contributions to output, and those who do not accept his results even as first approximations are those who deny the applicability of the connection. Second, it seems clear, if Denison's results can be accepted with caution, that the part played by education can vary widely from time to time and from country to country, regardless of the rate of economic growth. Finally, a large proportion of growth remains unexplained. From Table 5-2, for example, it can be seen

---

readable summary of Denison's work, see O'Donoghue, *Economic Dimensions of Education* pp. 107-109. Also, because of the wide variance of his results with those of Denison's, see Hector Correa, *The Economics of Human Resources* (Amsterdam: North-Holland, 1963), p. 172.

[g]Nicholas Kaldor, for example, argued that the extreme conditions of "perfect" competition and the absence of "external" economies were basic but unfulfilled assumptions of Denison's assumption that income received is a measure of the contribution to output which a particular factor makes. Also, he argued that labor's marginal product exceeds its average product because short-run fluctuations in employment are accompanied by more than proportional fluctuations in output, and therefore cannot have anything to do with its share in incomes. See Nicholas Kaldor, "Comments on Mr. Ingvar Svennilson's Paper," *The Residual Factor and Economic Growth,* pp. 138-43.

[h]Denison allocated 60 percent of higher earnings to education and 40 percent as an adjustment for other influences such as ability. He has not been convincing in arguing that this assumption flows from any plausible data.

that two-fifths to three-fourths of national income cannot be explained (see column 8). We are still at a loss to explain the real dynamics of economic growth, and the specter of an uncomfortably large residual persists.

Education and Economic Growth: Some Unanswered Questions

Obviously, much remains to be done in identifying and measuring the sources of economic growth and the influence of education on the contribution of labor to economic growth. Three examples may be cited as being particularly in need of serious study—study which could contribute worthwhile inputs to policy makers.

1. *Education Mix:* Mary Jean Bowman has stressed an idea that may prove important in the education literature, namely, that studies to date have ignored the effect of distribution of educational attainment on per capita income.[19]

2. *Skill as Adaptation and Innovation:* Bowman (et al.[20]), in particular, also has stressed for some time that the essence of growth is that it is a dynamic process, and that the role of education in economic growth lies in preparation for learning and adaptation in order to participate effectively in that growth. It has been suggested that education, by raising the level of adaptability, provides for a rapid diffusion of improved technologies and may explain why the supply of, and demand for, college-trained persons have moved together in the 1960s. In other words, technical change calls for a relatively high level of rapid learning and adaptation, the capability of which may be adduced by college certification or so it is held in the "conventional wisdom." We need to test these hypotheses.

3. *Productivity "Externalities:"* One source of imprecision in the type of studies which have been undertaken to date is productivity externalities. In short, especially where production is the result of highly organized human activity, the education of one worker may have favorable effects on the productivity of fellow workers. Such "education" is not caught by measurements of the Denison type.

Summary and Conclusion

Education clearly has important economic dimensions which render it a proper subject for economic analysis. Theodore Schultz recognized this a decade ago when he first began focusing attention upon the investment characteristic of education. The widespread acceptance of this characteristic has resulted in the kinds of economic research summarized in this report. Rate-of-return analysis, benefit-cost analysis, and measurements of the impact on the incomes of particular individuals and the society as a whole are the main examples of this.

The policy implications are far reaching. If economic efficiency is truly an important consideration in determining resource allocation in general and specifically with education, then the findings provided by economists are crucial to private and public decision-making. The evidence suggests, for example, that higher education shows a fairly stable payoff over time of about 15 percent, which is very similar to the rate of return on investment in the economy taken in its entirety. High school, on the other hand, appears to show a rising rate of return since World War II, upward of 25 percent for white males, while elementary schooling has been yielding well over 35 percent.

The comparison of the actual allocations with their respective rates of return clearly indicates some serious misallocation in our economic society. Permitting our human capital to deteriorate, maldistributing our educational investments because of social and institutional practices and arrangements, and especially overt and covert racial and sexual discrimination which results in inferior schooling and inferior job opportunities—all of these have distorted our educational investment decisions. Hard data may help correct these distortions resulting in redirections which would be not only more efficient but also more socially desirable.

6

Education and International Trade

The Microeconomic Aspects

In an open economy, the repercussions of domestic public policy decisions on the rest of the world must be considered. Micro effects on individual firms, industries, and their workers as well as macro effects on national income and prices influence the international relations of countries. This point is especially true for educational investment decisions because education, in many more ways than most other sectors, does effect the welfare of society. A special analysis of this process is required before a full understanding of education's unique effect on the economy can be attained.

The fact that educational investment and human capital, in general, explain a significant part of the growth of a nation's income and the productivity and standard of living of its people in itself does not justify a special study of the effects of education on a country's international trade.[1] In principle, it is not the level of productivity or growth in income of one country vis-à-vis the other that determines international trade patterns; it is the international differences in various industries that determines comparative advantage. And comparative advantage, not absolute advantage, is the basis for trade. The macro effects are important for the balance-of-payments considerations, but domestic economic policy should not be predicated upon balance-of-payments repercussions. There are other simpler and more efficient ways to handle balance-of-payments problems.[a]

This chapter, then, is mainly concerned with the micro effects of education. Education affects different sectors of the economy unequally, thereby providing a basis for comparative advantage. The unequal effects are the result of using education, or human capital, in different proportions in the production of different commodities. Thus the theory of human capital sheds light on the factors determin-

---

[a]Flexible exchange rates, a crawling peg, or even a policy of "benign neglect" would all be better presumably than a system which makes domestic policy a function of the international sector.

77

ing a country's structure of trade, and indeed, it was the explicit recognition of education and human capital's role in this process that saved international trade theory from the attacks on it that followed the discovery of the Leontief paradox.[b]

But again, other than furthering our understanding of comparative advantage, the human capital explanation of international trade holds few implications for public policy unless the externalities generated by different industries differ in a systematic way, or unless balance-of-payments considerations are deemed to be of major importance. A country's welfare, in principle, is not affected by whether it exports cloth or wine, steel or wheat, or computers or textiles unless externalities or spillovers are significant. These spillovers could include balance-of-payment effects under certain conditions.

Although there are no known studies comparing the positive and negative spillovers of our major industries, a priori it appears that many physical capital, unskilled labor, and natural-resource-intensive industries generate more pollution than the "clean" human-capital-intensive industries. The human-capital-intensive industries are probably more strategic from a national defense point of view, in addition to being a frequent source of national pride and export surplus. Thus, given a world of separate political divisions, the major powers are likely to pursue national goals of maintaining and encouraging their high technology sectors. Educational policy planners must consider, therefore, the repercussions of their decisions on the industrial and trade composition of the economy. That the United States takes these factors into account is apparent from official government publications.[2]

The Human-Capital Approach to Trade

The systematic way that education can be related to a country's commodity structure of trade is through the human capital and factor proportions theories. The factor proportions theory of international trade as developed by Heckscher, Ohlin, and Samuelson appeared to be in serious trouble when Leontief found, much to his

---

[b]Leontief discovered contrary to his expectation that U.S. exports were labor intensive and imports capital intensive. See Wassily W. Leontief, "Domestic Production and Foreign Trade: The American Capital Position Re-Examined," *Economica Internazionale* 7 (February 1954): 3-32.

surprise, that the United States, the relatively most physical capital abundant country in the world, was exporting not its capital-intensive commodities, as the factor proportions theory would predict, but its labor-intensive commodities.[3] Leontief himself, however, immediately turned to the quality of the labor force for the resolution of the paradox. The U. S. labor force was three times more efficient than foreign workers according to Leontief, and therefore, the United States was actually a labor abundant country.

Peter Kenen pointed out that the capital variable more aptly should be credited with the extra productivity of the U. S. labor force and that in reality the United States was total (human and physical) capital abundant.[4] This approach also dispatches the paradox, although not with quite the vigor human capital theorists had hoped.[c] Perhaps the reason is that capital is not quite as fungible between its human and physical forms as it should be before it is added together. Indeed, human-capital theorists are usually quick to point out the important differences between human and physical capital after discussing their basic similarities.[d]

A second approach to connect education with the factor proportions theory has been pursued by Donald Keesing.[5] This method simply considers human capital, or skilled labor, as a third factor of production and additionally minimizes the importance of physical capital because it flows freely across international boundaries and costs about the same in the major money markets of the world. Thus the human-capital or skilled-labor abundance of a country and the human-capital intensities of commodity production functions are thought to be the prime determinants of comparative advantage according to this line of reasoning.

Keesing proceeded by developing a skill index for labor working in the various industries and found that the aggregate index for the exports of countries with relatively abundant supplies of skilled labor tended to be high while the index for the country's imports was low. The results for thirteen countries and forty-six manufacturing industries are reproduced in Table 6-1. The importance of human capital in determining trade flows is exemplified by the -0.83 Spearman rank correlation coefficient between the export and import

---

[c]Only when the excess of wages of skilled labor over unskilled is capitalized by less than 12.7 percent is the paradox dispatched.

[d]And, of course, there are a few economists who do not believe that the concept of human capital is a useful or fruitful one. See H. Shaffer, "Investment in Human Capital: Comment," *American Economic Review* 52 (September 1961): 1026-1035.

Table 6-1

Skill Indices Associated with the Exports and Imports of Thirteen Countries

Country	Export Index[a]	Import Index[a]
United States	0.654	0.294
Sweden	0.547	0.431
Germany	0.541	0.345
United Kingdom	0.484	0.370
Switzerland	0.473	0.432
Canada	0.467	0.512
Netherlands	0.418	0.448
France	0.370	0.467
Austria	0.338	0.441
Belgium	0.323	0.441
Italy	0.293	0.554
Japan	0.281	0.737
India	0.084	0.554

[a]For computation on the skill index, see D. Keesing. The indices are based on 1960 U.S. skill requirements and the trade data is for forty-six manufacturing industries in 1962.

Source: Adapted from Tables 2 and 3, D. Keesing, "Labor Skills and the Structure of Trade in Manufactures," in P.B. Kenen and Roger Lawrence, eds., *The Open Economy* (New York: Columbia University Press, 1968), p. 14.

indices and by the 0.93 correlation coefficient between the export index and per capita income.[6] Countries with higher per capita income, and thus large stocks of human capital, tend to have their comparative advantages in industries which require relatively large amounts of skilled labor and their comparative disadvantages in industries which require relatively large amounts of unskilled labor.

The importance of human capital and labor skills in explaining United States trade patterns has also been substantiated recently by Robert Baldwin in an exhaustive survey of the empirical work in this area.[7] Baldwin found that when he added the costs of education (including foregone earnings as estimated by Schultz) to the costs of physical capital, U. S. exports were total capital intensive relative to imports when natural-resource-intensive industries were excluded. Another finding was that the average number of years of schooling completed was greater in export industries than import competing industries.[8]

Table 6-2 presents some evidence on the comparative advantage of specific United States industries and their physical capital, human capital, and labor-skill characteristics.[9] As an index of U. S. comparative advantage, exports minus competitive imports divided by shipments has been calculated for the twenty two-digit industries. The nonwages and salary value added per worker for each industry is presented as a measure of the flow of services from physical capital. Four proxies for human capital have been calculated for the twenty industries and these also appear in Table 6-2. They are: (1) wages and salary value added per worker; (2) the ratio of professional, technical, and kindred workers to total employment; (3) the median school years completed by males; and (4) the ratio of workers with five or more years of college to the total labor force. The Spearman and simple correlation coefficients between the trade performance index, and the factor intensity variables presented in Table 6-3 reveal that the human-capital variables perform significantly better than the physical-capital variables in explaining U. S. comparative advantage.

The above evidence indicates that the U. S. comparative advantage in machinery, chemicals, transportation equipment, and instruments evidently is based on the relative abundance of educated manpower in the United States, coupled with the high degree of human-capital requirements of these industries. It is also interesting to note that the highest levels of education appear to be the key to understanding commodity trade flows. In Table 6-3, the ratio of workers with five or more years of college has a slightly higher explanatory power than the median educational attainment of the work force. Baldwin also found that the U. S. exports differed more from U. S. import competing industries on the percentage of the embodied labor force that had some college than the percentage that were high school graduates.[10]

The highest skill categories of labor, such as professional and technical, have usually been able to "predict" comparative advantage better than less highly skilled categories, and as is indicated in Table 6-3, skill levels have generally performed better than formal education. These findings suggest that on-the-job training and experience supplement for formal educational investment as an explanation of commodity flows.[e] As Mincer has pointed out, on-the-job training is almost as large a human capital investment expenditure as formal education.[11] The findings on the importance of higher education and high skill levels are important because the social returns to

---

[e]Baldwin found that introducing several skill levels into his multiple regression equations improved the results; Baldwin, p. 137.

Table 6-2
Indices of Export Performance and Factor Intensity Variables for 1960

Industry	N-W&S	W&S	L-S[a]	M[b]	C[b]	X_1[c]
20 Food and kindred products	$ 6,700	$4,780	2.48%	10.4	.78%	-0.4
21 Tobacco products	14,860	3,870	2.18	9.5	.49	2.0
22 Textile mill products	2,740	3,570	1.90	8.7	.41	-2.0
23 Apparel and related products	2,110	3,130	1.10	10.1	.41	-0.9
24 Lumber and wood products	3,210	3,640	1.27	8.8	.37	-4.2
25 Furniture and fixtures	2,990	4,200	1.96	9.4	.49	0.2
26 Paper and allied products	8,930	5,380	5.07	10.8	1.35	-4.1
27 Printing and publishing	4,620	5,580	9.16	11.6	2.17	0.6
28 Chemicals and allied products	13,790	6,120	15.65	12.2	5.28	5.7
29 Petroleum and coal products	13,230	6,690	15.07	12.3	4.51	-1.0
30 Rubber and plastic products	4,690	5,280	5.79	11.2	1.82	0.4
31 Leather and leather products	2,280	3,570	.87	9.1	.39	-1.8
32 Stone, clay and glass products	5,720	5,050	4.96	9.9	1.19	-0.3
33 Primary metal industries	5,160	6,140	5.60	10.1	1.17	-0.5
34 Fabricated metal products	4,330	5,150	9.66	11.2	1.92	1.4
35 Machinery except electrical	4,170	5,930	9.38	11.6	1.60	9.6
36 Electrical machinery	4,360	5,390	15.23	12.3	3.19	2.6
37 Transportation equipment	5,040	6,510	12.19	11.5	2.20	3.9
38 Instruments and related products	5,350	5,920	16.18	12.3	3.67	3.3
39 Miscellaneous manufacturing	3,640	5,330	3.27	10.7	1.03	-1.8

[a]L-S is the percentage of professional, technical and kindred workers to total employment and is from *The U.S. Census of Population: 1960,* "Occupation by Industry."

[b]M and C are the median school years completed by males and the percentage of workers having completed five years of college to total workers for each industry, respectively. These indices were computed from *The U.S. Census of Population: 1960,* "Industrial Characteristics," PC (2)-7F.

[c]X_1 is calculated by subtracting imports from exports and dividing by shipments. Shipments have been taken from the *Annual Survey of Manufactures.* Exports and Imports came from *U.S. Commodity Exports & Imports as Related to Output, 1959 and 1960.*

Source: N-W&S and W&S are value added minus wages and salary divided by total employees for each industry and wages and salary divided by total employment, respectively. The data is from *The Annual Survey of Manufactures, 1959 and 1960.*

Table 6-3
Spearman and Simple Linear Correlation Coefficients between U.S. Export Performance and Various Indices of Factor Intensity (1960)

	Spearman	Simple Linear
N-W&S	0.311	0.190
W&S	0.467[a]	0.471[a]
L-S	0.675[b]	0.589[b]
M	0.612[b]	—
C	0.641[b]	0.470[a]

[a]Significant at the 0.05 level.
[b]Significant at the 0.01 level.
Source: Morrall, p. 41.

higher education usually have been judged to be lower than the social returns to (say) high school. Indeed, some writers have intimated that the social returns to higher education are negative.[f] To the extent that maintaining a comparative advantage in these industries as a national or "social" goal, governmental investment in higher education is supported by the human-capital approach to international trade.

The Neotechnology Theories

The human-capital theorists were almost as quick to embrace the foreign trade applications of their theory as the orthodox trade theorists were to adopt the concept of human capital to develop their neofactor proportions theories.[g] However, just as the relevance of the human-capital approaches to the study of education and the distribution of income have recently been called into question, the validity of the neofactor proportions theory of trade has been contested recently.[12] The human-capital theory of trade was not attacked for failure to withstand empirical testing; on the contrary, as reported above, the empirical support has been almost unanimous. The skepticism of the orthodox trade theory that arose after Leontief's findings was never quite dispelled by the neofactor proportions explanations. The assumptions of perfect competition, and

[f]James M. Buchanan makes this point in his discussion of the "new barbarians." See Buchanan and N. Deuletoglou, *Academia in Anarchy* (New York: Basic Books, 1970).

[g]G. Becker claimed that the human-capital concept could explain the Leontief paradox in his book, *Human Capital* (New York: Columbia University Press, 1964), pp. 59-60.

identical international production and demand conditions of the neofactor proportions theory flew in the face of observers of international economic relations.

The differences in technology or production function explanations have a long history in international trade theory. Indeed, the classical theory is based on differences in labor productivity among countries. Posner and Vernon were among the first to develop the neotechnology theory of trade,[13] in at least a semiformal approach. Lags and leads in technology are the basis for comparative advantage according to this explanation. To explain the comparative advantage of the United States, Vernon's product cycle theory introduces the concepts of stages of product development, imperfect competition and product differentiation, internal and external economies of scale, uncertainty and risk, and systematic differences in demand among countries.

Because the United States has the highest per capita income and the highest labor costs in the world, new income elastic and labor-saving products and processes will be developed first for the U. S. market. Due to information costs and the need for rapid communication between the marketer and the manufacturer of new unstandardized products, and due to the external economies available in the United States, the product will be produced first in the United States. Eventually, as the product becomes standardized, new competitors enter the field, and production costs become more important than marketing costs, so the product is produced overseas and eventually exported to the United States.

The intuitive appeal of this theory is matched by its empirical support. The empirical support for the neotechnology theories has been perhaps even more affirmative than the strong support for the neofactor proportions theory.[14] Usually using R & D as a percentage of sales of an industry or scientists and engineers engaged in R & D as a percentage of the labor force as proxies for the propensity to develop new products, several writers have found strong correlations between these indices and measures of the United States comparative advantage.[15]

Table 6-4 presents two proxies for the neotechnology variables, the percentage of the labor force that is scientists and engineers engaged in research and development and the rate of growth of the industry as measured by the percentage increase in value added

Table 6-4

Spearman and Simple Linear Correlation Coefficients between U.S. Export Performance and Various Neotechnology Indices (1960)

	Spearman	Simple Linear
S & E	0.613[a]	0.619[a]
VA	0.705[a]	0.543[a]

[a]Indiciates significance at the .01 level.

Source: Morrall, p. 52.

between 1947 and 1965.[h] The later variable is predicated on the assumption that new industries are usually growing more rapidly than mature and standardized industries. The correlations with the index for 1960 U. S. comparative advantage are slightly higher than were the similar correlations for the neofactor proportions variables.

Of course, there is no reason why these two models could not be combined, because the neofactor proportions model is a supply-side explanation, while the neotechnology theory emphasizes the demand side and has the additional advantage of taking into account the time dimension. Indeed, several studies that have combined the models through multiple regression analysis have found a significant improvement in the explained variance.[16] These positive findings for both theories, though, have led several writers to suggest that an eclectic approach to trade theory is appropriate.[17]

Although the acceptance of the "eclectic approach" reduces the importance of the human capital explanation somewhat, perhaps a greater threat to the theory lies in the validity of one of its basic assumptions. The neofactor proportions theory is based on the line of reasoning that a physically abundant factor produces a comparative advantage in products intensive in that factor because the physically abundant factor is also the "economically" abundant factor. In other words, a demand bias for that factor must not have caused that factor's price to have risen enough to have turned the physically abundant factor into an "economically" scarce factor.[18] In the human capital context, the question is whether the United States

---

[h]The following empirical evidence is from Morrall, *Human Capital*. Various comparable time spans for the value-added variable and years other than 1960 for the export variable were tried with results similar to those reported.

Table 6-5
International Comparison of the Economic Abundance of Human Capital

Countires	Relative Abundance[a]
Japan	1.44
Norway	2.10
Israel	2.10
Netherlands	2.21
United Kingdom	2.24
Phillipines	2.24
Greece	2.24
India	2.38
United States	2.40
Canada	2.44
France	2.55
Mexico	3.08
Chile	4.40
Colombia	4.50
Kenya	5.29
Ghana	9.31
Nigeria	9.46
Uganda	12.21

[a]Wages of workers with twelve or more years of education divided by the wages of workers with zero to seven years of education. Calculated from date in G. Psacharopoulos and K. Hinchliffe, "Further Evidence of Substitution among Different Types of Educated Labor," *Journal of Political Economy* 80 (July 1972): 788.

demand for human capital has resulted in a demand reversal, that is, has the tremendous United States private and governmental demand for human capital resulted in human capital being relatively higher priced in the U. S. than in our major trading partners? This is a difficult question to answer because comparable international data on skill differentials, rates of return to human capital, or the variances in occupational wage distributions are scarce and untrustworthy. However, the only study that has directly addressed this question found that, indeed, U. S. human capital is relatively higher compensated than in most other developed nations.[19]

Recent data developed by Psacharopoulos and Hinchliffe have been used to rank countries on their "economic" human capital abundance.[20] Table 6-5 shows that the United States falls in the middle of the rankings of eighteen countries for which data were available on the basis of the wages of workers with twelve or more years of education relative to the wages of workers with zero to seven years. These data indicate that the human-capital explanation of trade is logically incorrect at least according to orthodox reasoning.

The explanation for the correlation between human-capital intensity and export performance might simply be due to the heavy requirements for human capital in the development of new products. Instead of the abundant U. S. supply of human capital being the basis for U. S. exports, perhaps the demand for new products and the derived demand for human capital created the huge relative numerical abundance of skilled workers observed for the United States.

A successful discussion of the role of education in trade theory must explain not only why U. S. exports tend to be intensive in human capital but also why this situation can co-exist with the skilled manpower shortage in the United States that was evident during the fifties and sixties. A complicated neofactor proportions theory can be invoked to explain the above empirical findings. First, if physical capital and human capital are complementary, as several economists have suggested,[21] and, given that the United States does have an apparent physical abundance of human capital, then high U. S. relative international skill differentials can be explained. But this complementarity would mean that U. S. exports should be tangible capital intensive as well as human-capital intensive, a finding contradicted by Leontief and others. The factor proportions explanation may still be rescued by further hypothesizing that the scarcest factor of U. S. production is natural resources which dominates our trade picture, and, when combined with a strong complementarity between physical capital and natural resources, explains the Leontief paradox. But this list of ad hoc assumptions and speculations leaves one uncomfortable. Expanding this list of factors of production to four or more begins to change the model from theory to description.

Because the neotechnology theory easily explains these phenomena without further modifications, the findings on skill differentials and human capital scarcity must be counted as support for the neotechnology theories. If this is true, the question arises as to the role of human capital in explaining trade patterns. If education is important in determining growth, the distribution of income, and many other economic phenomena, one also would expect it to be an important factor in determining a nation's comparative advantage. The intention of the above arguments has not been to summarily dismiss the factor of proportions theory of trade, only to call it into question. Probably human capital as a factor of production is important, but it is not the prime determinant of U. S. comparative advantage. However, human capital may still be the prime determinant of comparative advantage because human capital also plays the key role in the neotechnology model.

Education and the Neotechnology Theory

A higher relative return to skilled labor and exports of human-capital-intensive products is not inconsistent with the neotechnology theory which does not posit similar production functions, constant returns to scale, and the absence of externalities and imperfect competition. On the contrary, since new products and processes are likely to be both human and physical capital intensive, and produced under imperfect competition, the neotechnology theory actually predicts these results.

The development of new products and processes is itself a form of educational capital. The discoveries involve present sacrifices which give rise to a future stream of increased earnings, while the processes of invention and innovation are themselves a special kind of education that involves learning new knowledge rather than old. One may argue that formal education does not necessarily lead to technological advancement, but technological advancement is by definition a form of education. Because formal education, on-the-job training or experience, and the acquiring of information new to society, however, are probably all complementary, then all forms of education can be said to promote technological change.

Bowman and Nelson and Phelps have emphasized the importance of education in increasing the flexibility and adaptability of the labor force. They argue that education serves to reduce the time lags between the discovery of new knowledge, innovation, and widespread imitation.[22] And Welch has provided the empirical support for the proposition that formal education acts more than just as an augmentation of a factor of production. It also increases the efficiency with which the factors of production are allocated, especially when technological change is rapid.[23] In effect, this function of education improves "X" or technical efficiency.[24] Thus it is almost a tautology to say that educational investment increases invention, innovation, and imitation, that is, produces technological change. The statement is not quite a tautology because demand is also important.

But educational investment also plays a role on the demand side. Anne Krueger has found that under conservative assumptions, more than half of the differences in per capita incomes between the United States and the less developed countries is due to differences in their endowments of human capital. [25] According to the neotechnology theory, the higher per capita income of the United States is the driving force which causes the United States to produce first the new income elastic products and processes. Thus education has the interesting characteristic of providing much of its own demand; a characteristic which helps to explain why the demand for education more than kept pace with the tremendous expansion in the number of high school and college graduates in the United States in the fifties and the sixties. [26]

Another aspect of the neotechnology theory of trade is the proposition that economies of scale, especially on high technology industries, may be important in explaining comparative advantage. Both Kenen and Keesing point out the economies of scale in the production of educational capital may be particularly important in explaining a sustained advantage in human-capital intensive products. [27] Because educational capital is the most important input in the production of education capital itself and because the opportunity costs of human capital decline as the stock of human capital increases, additional amounts of schooling and training can be produced at declining costs. This phenomenon should be true for firms producing "specific" (in the Becker sense) human capital as well as formal educational establishments.

Finally, education produces externalities that accrue to other workers both in the same firm and in other firms related to the first, either horizontally or vertically. Weisbrod has described the employment-related benefits of education and pointed out that these are a function of the extent of imperfect competition and the extent that one's formal education is "specific" to a particular firm. [28] In these cases, a firm may be able to pay workers less than their marginal product. These phenomena seem particularly likely in the high technology industries where imperfect competition is strong and where engineers and scientists tend to be highly specialized with only a few prospective employers.

Outside firms will also benefit because communication costs are reduced by having an educated work force. Vernon emphasized communication costs between firms as a function of distance as a major factor in determining why new products would be manufactured in the United States despite relatively higher labor costs. Communication costs as a function of education also should be emphasized.

The roles of education in producing technological progress, economies of scale, and externalities internal and external to the firm help explain the co-existence of the U. S. comparative advantage in skill-intensive products and the relatively high skill differentials of the United States vis-à-vis her main trading partners. Presumably, the relative marginal productivity of U. S. human capital is even higher.

Education, then, appears to be the key element in the neotechnology theories of trade, just as it is in the neofactor proportions model. The international trade repercussions of educational investment decisions do not hinge upon which theory is the main explanation of U. S. comparative advantage. Both theories give the same policy prescriptions. Given the goal to promote high technology or human-capital-intensive industries in an open and free economy, educational investment should be supported for these reasons by the government.

However, the different theories do prescribe emphasis on different educational investments. In particular, the neotechnology theory points out the importance of higher education and doctoral and postdoctoral research, while the neofactor proportions theory makes no distinction between the different kinds of levels of education. This is an important distinction because most of the other social benefits claimed for education are thought to be more important at the primary and secondary levels than at the postsecondary level.

U. S. Educational Policy and International Trade

The ways that the United States government has influenced our international trade patterns may be analyzed through the use of these two theories. Although U. S. educational investment expanded tremendously in the post-World War II period increasing from 3.7 percent of GNP in 1955 to 6.3 percent in 1969,[29] supply did not keep up with demand as the median income of workers with college educations increased from 198 percent to 254 percent of the median income for grade school educated workers over the period

1949 to 1969.[30] This development can be attributed to the tremendous increase in governmental defense and space R & D. There was an eighteen-fold increase in federal expenditures for R & D for defense, AEC, and NASA combined between 1948 and 1964.[31]

Thus, from the supply side, this pressure on net undermined our comparative advantage in human capital despite the increased financial support for education. From the demand side, however, new technologies were developed from which comparative advantages sprung. But since the favored industries were quite few and specialized, it is problematical that the combined effect strengthened our comparative advantage. Certainly, the neglected sectors were hard pressed to develop or maintain comparative advantages. An implicit recognition of this phenomenon appears in the 1972 *Economic Report of the President* and the *Budget of the United States Government: FY 1973*. Both documents call for expanded support for R & D, especially emphasizing the previously neglected fields of energy, the environment, transportation, health, natural disasters, and drugs. In fact, the FY 73 budget calls for a 15 percent increase for civilian R & D.[32]

The recent decline in national defense expenditures as a percentage of GNP has also reduced the relative price rises for human capital and should help restrengthen the U. S. comparative advantage in human-capital-intensive products through the neofactor proportions mechanisms. The new Higher Education Act of 1972 reaffirms the federal government's support of education after the recent pause and thus, from both neofactor proportions and neotechnology reasoning will promote the United States comparative advantage in high technology industry. The FY 73 budget recommendation for education and manpower is 43 percent above the 1971 actual expenditure.[33]

The effect of these steps, of course, may not show up in the trade statistics for several years. And it may very well be that a major shift has occurred because of the slowdown in the growth of our economy and in the support for education and R & D that occurred in the late sixties. These past events should be more damaging according to neotechnology than neofactor proportions reasoning. In fact, these changes, to the extent that they held down skilled labor costs, may even have stimulated our advantages in human-capital-intensive industries according to the latter theory's propositions. Of course, the U. S. comparative advantage depends not just on U. S. conditions but depends equally on conditions in other countries. Thus the recent policy steps must be viewed in light of our main trading partners' actions.

No one trade theory has emerged as the dominant one, and most economists still believe that an eclectic approach is appropriate, and that the best policy approach is the one the United States evidently has decided to follow, namely, to operate as if both theories were correct. In this instance, this procedure can be followed because the policy prescriptions are not in conflict. Even though recently the weight of evidence has been on the neotechnology side, there is reason to expect that human capital as a factor of production might increase in importance over time as international communication and technological diffusion speed up. And economists are happier when both supply and demand count.

Notes

Chapter 1
The Concept of Investment in Education

1. Fritz Machlup, *Education and Economic Growth*, (Lincoln, Nebr.: University of Nebraska Press, 1970), p. 5. Also see Machlup's earlier book, *The Production and Distribution of Knowledge in the United States* (Princeton, N.J.: Princeton University Press, 1962), pp. 108-110, 115.

2. Theodore W. Schultz, "Investment in Human Capital," *American Economic Review* 51 (December 1961): 1-17; and "Reflections on Investment in Man," *Journal of Political Economy* 70 (Supplement: October 1962): 1-8; also Gary Becker, "Investment in Human Capital: A Theoretical Analysis," *Journal of Political Economy* 70 (Supplement: October 1962): 9-50; and *Human Capital*, (New York: National Bureau of Economic Research, 1964).

3. Anne O. Krueger, "Factor Endowment and Per Capita Income Differences Among Countries," *The Economic Journal* 78 (September 1968): 641-59.

4. See Theodore W. Schultz, "The Human Capital Approach to Education," *Economic Factors Affecting the Financing of Education,* Roe Johns, Irving Goffman, Kern Alexander, and Dewey Stollar, eds. (Gainesville, Fla.: National Educational Finance Project, 1970), p. 35.

5. See George J. Stigler, "Information in the Labor Market," *The Journal of Political Economy* 70 (Supplement: October 1962): 94-105.

6. Finis Welch, "Labor Market Discrimination: An Interpretation of Income Differences in the Rural South," *The Journal of Political Economy* 75 (June 1967): 225-40.

7. This discussion is based on Schultz, "The Human Capital Approach to Education," pp. 18-19.

Chapter 2
Educational Investment and Resource Allocation

1. The discussion of economic and social spillovers follows

very closely: J. Ronnie Davis, "The Social and Economic Externalities of Education," *Economic Factors Affecting the Financing of Education*, Roe Johns, Irving Goffman, Kern Alexander, and Dewey Stollard, eds. (Gainesville: National Education Finance Project, 1970), pp. 59-81.

2. For example, see U.S. Department of Labor, *Manpower Report of the President* (Washington: U.S. Printing Office, 1970), p. 167.

3. A start on developing a framework for analyzing the future demand for education has been made by Kenneth E. Boulding, "Factors Affecting the Future Demand for Education," *Economic Factors Affecting the Financing of Education*, pp. 1-28.

4. For an exposition of this position, see Ivar Berg, *The Great Training Robbery* (New York: Praeger Publishers, Inc., 1970).

5. For a strong criticism of Berg's position, see Mary Jean Bowman, "Education and Economic Growth," *Economic Factors Affecting the Financing of Education*, pp. 105-110.

6. Milton Friedman and Simon Kuznets, *Incomes from Independent Professional Practice* (New York: National Bureau of Economic Research, 1945).

7. Burton A. Weisbrod, "Education and Investment in Human Capital," *Journal of Political Economy* 70 (Supplement: October 1962): 106-23; *External Benefits of Public Education* (Princeton, N.J.: Industrial Relations Section, Department of Economics, Princeton University, 1964). Also, for a very similar study, see Werner Z. Hirsch et al., *Spillover of Education Costs and Benefits* (Los Angeles: Institute of Government and Public Affairs, UCLA, 1964).

8. Weisbrod, "Education and Investment in Human Capital."

9. Martin O'Donoghue, *Economic Dimensions of Education* (Chicago: Aldine-Antheneum, 1971).

10. Weisbrod, *External Benefits of Public Education*, p. 29.

11. Burton A. Weisbrod and William J. Swift, "On the Monetary Value of Education's Intergeneration Effects," *Journal of Political Economy* 73 (December 1965): 643-49.

12. Finis Welch, "Education in Production," *Journal of Political Economy* 78 (January-February 1970): 35-59.

13. Ibid., p. 36.

14. Ibid., p. 55.

15. Weisbrod, *External Benefits of Public Education*, pp. 30-31.

16. Ibid., p. 32.   .

17. See Hirsch et al., *Spillover of Education Costs*, p. 336.

18. O'Donoghue, *Economic Dimensions*, p. 92.

19. Weisbrod, *External Benefits of Public Education*, pp. 32-34.

20. Economic and other barriers also might be removed from education and training *themselves*. See James S. Coleman: "Equal Schools or Equal Students," *The Public Interest* 1 (Summer 1966): 72.

21. See Weisbrod, *External Benefits of Public Education*, p. 133; and Carl S. Shoup, *Public Finance* (Chicago: Aldine, 1969), p. 133.

22. For example, see Paul L. Dressel, "Comments on the Use of Mathematical Models in Educational Planning," *Mathematical Models in Educational Planning* (Paris: OECD, 1967), pp. 275-88.

23. Shoup, *Public Finance*, p. 97.

24. Weisbrod, *External Benefits of Public Education*, p. 31.

25. Charles A. Benson, *The Economics of Public Education* (Boston: Houghton Mifflin, Inc., 1961), p. 145.

26. Fritz Machlup, *Education and Economic Growth* (Lincoln, Nebr.: University of Nebraska Press, 1970), pp. 55-56.

27. E.G. West, *Education and the State* (London: Institute of Economic Affairs, 1965); and *Economics, Education and the Politician* (London: Institute of Economic Affairs, 1968).

28. West, *Education and the State*, p. 36.

29. O'Donoghue, *Economic Dimensions*, p. 90.

30. Jack Wiseman, "Cost Benefit Analysis in Education," *Southern Economic Journal* 32 (Supplement: July 1965): 1-14.

31. Simon Kuznets, "Economic Growth and Income Inequality," *American Economic Review* 45 (March 1955): 1-28; and "Quantitative Aspects of Economic Growth VII," *Economic Development and Cultural Change* (January 1963): 1-80.

32. Paul Samuelson, *Economics* (New York: McGraw-Hill Book Company, 1970), pp. 112-13. However, Samuelson also points out that income inequality has not declined in the United States since 1945, this despite a phenomenal rise in average education over this period. See Welch, "Education in Production," p. 36.

33. Thomas I. Ribich, "The Effect of Educational Spending on Poverty Reduction," *Economic Factors Affecting the Financing of Education*, pp. 207-208.

34. Ibid., pp. 208-33.

35. Thomas I. Ribich, *Education and Poverty* (Washington: Brookings, 1968), pp. 34-99, also Ibid., pp. 226-30.

36. Ribich, "The Effect of Educational Spending on Poverty Reduction," pp. 230-31.

37. B.R. Chiswick, "The Average Level of Schooling and the Intra-Regional Inequality of Income: A Clarification," *American Economic Review* 58 (June 1968): 495-500.

38. Ibid., p. 495.

39. Edward Denison, "An Aspect of Inequality of Opportunity," *Journal of Political Economy* 78 (September-October 1970): 1195-1202.

40. Ibid., p. 1199.

41. See Roland N. McKean, "The Use of Shadow Prices," *Problems in Public Expenditure Analysis*, Samuel B. Chase, Jr., ed. (Washington: Brookings, 1968), pp. 33-37.

42. See Roland N. McKean, *Public Spending* (New York: McGraw-Hill), pp. 128-29.

43. Weisbrod, *External Benefits of Public Education*.

44. Hirsch et al., *Spillover of Education Costs*.

45. Hirsch et al., dispute this. They argue that spillovers lead to underinvestment in some instances and to overinvestment in others. Hirsch et al., *Spillover of Education Costs*, p. 414.

46. R. Malul, "Review of B.A. Weisbrod, 'External Benefits of Public Education'," *Journal of Political Economy* 73 (December 1965): 667-68.

47. A.G. Holtman, "A Note on Public Education and Spillovers through Migration," *Journal of Political Economy* 74 (October 1966): 524-25.

48. A. Williams, "The Optimal Provision of Public Goods in a System of Local Government," *Journal of Political Economy* 74 (February 1966): 18-33.

49. See James M. Buchanan, *The Public Finances* (Homewood, Ill.: Irwin, 1970), pp. 417-32.

50. For a summary of alternative adjustments, see Otto A. Davis and Morton I. Kamien, "Externalities, Information and Alternative Collective Action," *Public Expenditures and Policy Analysis*, Robert H. Haveman and Julius Margolis, eds. (Chicago: Markham Publishing Company, 1970), pp. 74-95.

51. Two strong advocates of such a scheme are Friedman and Buchanan. See Milton Friedman, *Capitalism and Freedom* (Chicago: University of Chicago Press, 1962); and James M. Buchanan and Nicos E. Devletoglou, *Academia in Anarchy* (New York: Basic Books, 1970).

52. See John D. Owen, "Education for Majority Voting?" *Public Choice* 6 (Spring 1969): 65-66.

53. Mark V. Pauly, "Mixed Public and Private Financing of Education: Efficiency and Feasibility," *American Economic Review* 57 (March 1967): 120-30.

54. James M. Buchanan and William Craig Stubblebine, "Externality," *Economica* 29 (November 1962): 371-84.

55. Paul A. Samuelson, "The Pure Theory of Public Expenditure," *Review of Economics and Statistics* 36 (November 1954): 387-89.

56. See Paul A. Samuelson, "Contrast between Welfare Conditions for Joint Supply and for Public Goods," *Review of Economics and Statistics* 51 (February 1969): 26-30.

Chapter 3
Educational Investment and the Valuation Problem

1. See Roland N. McKean, *Public Spending* (New York: McGraw-Hill), p. 135.

2. See J.V. Krutilla and Otto Eckstein, *Multiple Purpose River Development* (Baltimore: Johns Hopkins Press, 1958); and Otto Eckstein, *Water Resource Development* (Cambridge, Mass.: Harvard University Press, 1958).

3. Charles J. Hitch and Roland N. McKean, *The Economics of Defense in the Nuclear Age* (Cambridge, Mass.: Harvard University Press, 1960).

4. See Alan R. Prest and Ralph Turvey, "Cost-Benefit Analysis: A Survey," *Economic Journal* 75 (December 1965): 683-735.

5. Mary Jean Bowman, "Education and Economic Growth," *Economic Factors Affecting the Financing of Education*, Roe Johns, Irving Goffman, Kern Alexander, and Dewey Stollard, eds. (Gainsville, Fla.: National Educational Finance Project, 1970), pp. 87-88.

6. See McKean, *Public Spending*, p. 136. Also, see Selma J. Mushkin and William Pollak, "Analysis in a PPBS Setting," *Economic Factors Affecting the Financing of Education*, Roe Johns et al, eds. (Gainseville, Fla.: National Educational Finance Project, 1970), pp. 330-31.

7. This discussion follows very closely, Thomas I. Ribich, *Education and Poverty* (Washington, D. C.: Brookings, 1968).

8. Harold A. Gibbard and Gerald G. Somers, "Government Retraining of the Unemployed in West Virginia," *Retraining the Unemployed*, Gerald G. Somers, ed. (Madison, Wis.: University of Wisconsin Press, 1968), pp. 17-124.

9. Glen G. Cain and Ernst W. Stromsdorfer, "An Economic Evaluation of Government Retraining Programs in West Virginia," *Retraining the Unemployed*, pp. 299-335.

10. Gerald G. Somers and Ernst W. Stromsdorfer, "A Benefit-Cost Analysis of Manpower Retraining," *Proceedings of the Seventeenth Annual Meetings*, Gerald G. Somers, ed. (Madison, Wis.: Industrial Relations Research Association, 1965), pp. 172-85.

11. Ernst W. Stromsdorfer, "Determinants of Economic Success in Retraining the Unemployed," *Journal of Human Resources* 3 (Spring 1968): pp. 139-58.

12. Richard J. Solie, "Employment Effects of Retraining the Unemployed," *Industrial and Labor Relations Review* 21 (January 1968): pp. 210-25; and "An Evaluation of the Effects of Retraining in Tennessee," *Retraining the Unemployed*, pp. 193-211.

13. Michael E. Borus, "A Benefit-Cost Analysis of the Economic Effectiveness of Retraining the Unemployed," *Yale Economic Essays* 4 (Fall 1964): 371-429; "The Effects of Retraining the Unemployed in Connecticut," *Retraining the Unemployed*, pp. 125-148; and "Time Trends in the Benefits from Retraining in Con-

necticut,'' *Proceedings of the Twentieth Annual Winter Meetings* (Madison, Wis.: Industrial Relations Research Association, 1968), pp. 36-46.

14. David A. Page, ''Retraining under the Manpower Development Act: A Cost-Benefit Analysis,'' *Public Policy* 13 (1964): 257-76.

15. E. C. Gooding, *The Massachusetts Retraining Program, Statistical Supplement* (Boston: Federal Reserve Bank, 1962).

16. Einar Hardin and Michael E. Borus, ''An Economic Evaluation of the Retraining Program in Michigan: Methodological Problems of Research,'' *Proceedings of the 1966 Social Statistics Section Meetings* (Washington: American Statistical Association, 1966), pp. 133-37.

17. Earl D. Main, ''A Nationwide Evaluation of MDTA Institutional Job Training,'' *Journal of Human Resources* 3 (Spring 1968): 159-70.

18. Main, ''Nationwide Evaluation of MDTA,'' p. 159.

19. Ibid., p. 169.

20. Robert E. Hall, ''Prospects for Shifting the Phillips Curve through Manpower Policy,'' *Brookings Papers on Economic Activity* 3 (1971): 678.

21. Orley Ashenfelter, ''Progress Report on the Development of Certain Performance Information on the Impact of MDTA,'' Technical Analysis Paper, No. 12a, Office of Evaluation, Office of Assistant Secretary for Policy, Evaluation and Research, Department of Labor (April 1973), mimeo.

22. See Edward R. Fried et al., *Setting National Priorities: The 1974 Budget* (Washington, D.C.: Brookings, 1973), p. 222.

23. Resource Management Corporation, *Evaluations of the War on Poverty: The Feasibility of Benefit-Cost Analysis for Manpower Programs*, RMC Report UR-054, prepared for GAO (March 1969), Supplements 1 and 2.

24. Burton A. Weisbrod, ''Preventing High School Dropout,'' *Measuring Benefits of Government Investments*, Robert Dorfman, ed. (Washington: Brookings, 1965), pp. 117-149.

25. Gerald G. Somers and Ernst W. Stromsdorfer, ''Neighborhood Youth Corps: A Nationwide Analysis,'' *Journal of Human Resources* 7 (Fall 1972): 447-59.

26. Glen Cain, *Benefit Cost Estimates for Job Corps* (Madison, Wis.: Institute for Research on Poverty, University of Wisconsin, 1967).

27. Sample data on "no-shows" and those who completed Job Corps were gathered by the Louis Harris organization. See Louis Harris and Associates, *A Study of August 1966 Terminations from the Job Corps* (Washington, D.C.: Institute for Applied Technology, National Bureau of Standards, U. S. Department of Commerce, 1967).

28. Sar A. Levitan, *Antipoverty, Work and Training Efforts: Goals and Reality* (Ann Arbor and Detroit: Institute of Labor and Industrial Relations, University of Michigan-Wayne State University, 1967).

29. See V. Lane Rawlins, "Job Corps: The Urban Center as a Training Facility," *Journal of Human Resources* 6 (Spring 1971): 221-235. Rawlins concluded that "when trainees are able and willing to complete the training course, the program has a positive impact on earnings" (p. 234).

30. These points are made by Fried et al., *Setting National Priorities*, p. 223.

31. Ribich, *Education and Poverty*, pp. 61-78.

32. Ribich also lists several other reasons for these results. See, ibid., pp. 73-74.

33. Ibid., p. 77.

34. See E. J. Mosbeck et al., "Analyses of Compensatory Education in Five School Districts: Summary" (Santa Barbara, Calif.: General Electric Company, TEMPO, 1968).

35. Alice M. Rivlin, *Systematic Thinking for Social Action* (Washington D.C.: Brookings, 1971), pp. 79-85.

36. American Institutes for Research, *ESEA Title I: A Re-Analysis and Synthesis of Evaluation Data for FY 1965 through FY 1970* (Palo Alto, Calif;: March 1972).

37. Irwin Garfinkel and Edward Gramlich, "A Statistical Analysis of the OEO Experiment in Educational Performance Contracting," *Journal of Human Resources* (Summer 1973): 275-305.

38. Ibid., p. 304.

39. Ribich, *Education and Poverty*, pp. 78-80.

40. This approach is the one followed by Rivlin, See Rivlin, *Systematic Thinking*, pp. 69-85.

41. M. Blaug, "The Rate of Return on Investment in Education," M. Blaug, ed., *Economics of Education* (Baltimore: Penguin Books, 1968), p. 167.

42. Gary Becker, *Human Capital* (New York: NBER, 1964).

43. Ibid, pp. 78 and 120.

44. See D. W. Jorgenson and Z. Grillichs, "The Expansion of Productivity Change," *Review of Economic Studies* 34 (July 1967): 249-83.

45. Theodore W. Schultz, "The Human Capital Approach to Education," *Economic Factors Affecting the Financing of Education*, Roe Johns et al., eds. (Gainsville, Fla.: National Education Finance Project, 1970), p. 50.

46. Giora Hanoch, "Personal Earnings and Investment in Schooling," (Ph.D dissertation, University of Chicago, 1965); and "Personal Earnings and Investment in Schooling," *Journal of Human Resources* (Summer 1967): 310-329.

47. See W. Lee Hansen, "Total and Private Rates of Return to Investment in Schooling," *Journal of Political Economy* 71 (April 1963): 128-40.

48. See Daniel C. Rogers, "Private Rates of Return to Education in the United States: A Case Study," *Yale Economic Essays* 9 (Spring 1969): 89-134.

49. Ibid., pp. 127-128.

50. See Thomas Johnson, "Returns from Investment in Human Capital," *American Economic Review* 60 (September 1970): 546-60.

51. Ibid., p. 558.

52. Rogers, "Private Rates of Return," p. 124; also, see Shane Hunt, "Income Determinants for College Graduates and the Return to Educational Investment," *Yale Economic Essays* 3 (Fall 1963): 305-357; and Johnson, "Returns from Investment," p. 558.

53. Orley Ashenfelter and Joseph Mooney, "Some Evidence on the Private Returns to Graduate Education," *The Southern Economic Journal* 35 (January 1969): 247-56.

54. Schultz, "Human Capital Approach," p. 48.

55. Ibid., and Johnson, "Return from Investment," p. 558.

56. Schultz, "Human Capital Approach," p. 48.

57. For an excellent discussion of all the problems of estimating an educational production function and for one of the first attempts at doing so, see Samuel Bowles, "Towards an Educational Production Function," *Education, Income and Human Capital*, W. Lee Hansen, ed. (New York: National Bureau of Economic Research, 1970), pp. 11-70, and the discussion that follows.

58. Henry M. Levin, "The Effect of Different Levels of Expenditure on Educational Output," in Johns, et al., eds., pp. 173-206. This was also a conclusion of the "Coleman Report," see James S. Coleman et al., *Equality of Educational Opportunity*, O. E. 38001 (Washington: U. S. Office of Health, Education and Welfare, 1966). p. 316.

59. Henry M. Levin, "A Cost-Effectiveness Analysis of Teacher Selection," *Journal of Human Resources* 5 (Winter 1970): 24-33.

Chapter 4
Educational Investment and Discrimination

1. Gary Becker, *Human Capital* (New York: National Bureau of Economic Research, 1964), p. 94.

2. J. Gwartney, "Changes in the Nonwhite/White Income Ratio—1939-1967," *The American Economic Review* 60 (December 1970): 873.

3. Ibid., p. 874.

4. Gordon Allport, *The Nature of Prejudice* (Garden City, N.J.: Doubleday Anchor Books, 1958), p. 10.

5. For a statement of this view, see P. Black and R. Atkins, "Conformity versus Prejudice as Exemplified in White-Negro Relations in the South: Some Methodological Consideration," *Journal of Psychology* 30 (1950), pp. 109-21.

6. M. Friedman, *Capitalism and Freedom* (Chicago: Phoenix Books, 1965), p. 110.

7. Ibid., pp. 109-10.

8. Gary Becker, *The Economics of Discrimination* (Chicago: University of Chicago Press, 1957).

9. Ibid., p. 6.

10. Ibid., p. 5.

11. See ibid., for a discussion of the Heckscher-Ohlin model and the importance of education in the new Heckscher-Ohlin models.

12. For a division of the functional interpretation of prejudice, see D. Krech, R. Crutchfield, and E. Ballachy, *Individual in Society: A Textbook of Social Psychology* (New York: McGraw-Hill Book Company, Inc., 1962), pp. 182-86.

13. Becker, *The Economics of Discrimination*, pp. 11-16.

14. See the chapter, "Educational Investment and the U. S.'s Comparative Advantage in International Trade."

15. For a review of international trade theory, see A. Freeman, *International Trade, An Introduction to Method and Theory* (New York: Harper & Row, 1971).

16. Becker, *The Economics of Discrimination*, p. 15.

17. See W. Stolper and P. Samuelson, "Protection and Real Wages," *Review of Economic Studies* 9 (November 1941): 58-73.

18. Becker, *The Economics of Discrimination*, p. 13, and Baran and Sweezy, "Monopoly Capitalism and Race Relations," p. 271. For a Marxian criticism of Becker, see M. Silver, "Employee Tastes for Discrimination, Wages and Profits," *Review of Social Economy* 26 (September 1968): 183-85, who points out that discrimination also increases the costs of collusion of employees against management and thus increases capitalist profits.

19. See the studies cited in Krech, et al., *Individual in Society*, pp. 182-86.

20. Anne Krueger, "The Economics of Discrimination," *Journal of Political Economy* 71 (October 1963): 481-86.

21. See Harry Johnson, "Optimum Tariffs and Retaliation," *International Trade and Economic Growth* (Cambridge, Mass.: Harvard University Press, 1958).

22. Krueger, "Economics of Discrimination," p. 483.

23. Gwartney, "Discrimination and Income Differentials," pp. 396-409. Gwartney provides upper and lower bounds for his index number estimates. Here the ranges have been averaged to simplify the presentation.

24. Ibid., p. 402.

25. This figure and the following aggregate estimates were calculated by the authors by applying Gwartney's estimates to national income figures for 1960 as found in the U. S. Bureau of the Census, *Statistical Abstract of the United States-1966*, 87th ed. (Washington, D.C.: 1966).

26. L. Thurow estimates with completely different techniques that the white distribution gain in 1960 from discrimination was $15 billion while the inefficiency loss was $18.8 billion. The similarity to our estimates is startling. See L. Thurow, *Poverty and Discrimination* (Washington, D.C.: Brookings, 1969), pp. 130-37.

27. A more accurate estimate must await the arrival of the 1970 census data.

28. The previously cited estimates of Thurow support this view. Also, P. Samuelson has expressed this belief in his *Economics* (New York: McGraw-Hill, 1970), p. 783. The $11.625 billion difference in 1960 is due to the lower level of education and achievement of blacks and represents an inefficiency loss while the $7.125 billion due to job discrimination entails both distribution and efficiency effects.

29. F. Welch, "Labor-Market Discrimination: An Interpretation of Income Differences in the Rural South," *The Journal of Political Economy* 75 (June 1967): 239.

30. For a discussion of the correct specification of human-capital production function, see L. Thurow, *Investment in Human Capital* (Belmont, Calif.: Wadsworth Publishing Co., 1970), pp. 53-64.

31. T. Johnson, "Returns from Investment in Human Capital," *American Economic Review* 60 (September 1970): 557-58.

32. R. Weiss, "The Effect of Education on the Earnings of Blacks and Whites," *The Review of Economics and Statistics* 52 (May 1970): 150-59.

33. Ibid., p. 159.

Chapter 5
Educational Investment and Economic Growth

1. William G. Bowen and T. Aldrich Finegan, *The Economics of Labor Force Participation* (Princeton, N.J.: Princeton University Press, 1969), pp. 53-62.

2. See W. Arthur Lewis, "Education and Economic Development," *Readings in the Economics of Education,* ed. Mary Jean Bowman et al. (Paris: UNESCO, 1968), pp. 135-45. Also, for international comparisons of education, labor, and economic growth, see Frederick Harbison and Charles A. Myers, *Education, Manpower and Economic Growth* (New York: McGraw-Hill, 1964).

3. See John Maynard Keynes, *The General Theory of Employment, Interest and Money* (New York: Harcourt, Brace & Co. 1936).

4. See Roy Harrod, "An Essay in Dynamic Theory," *Economic Journal* 49 (March 1939): 14-33; and Evsey D. Domar, "Capital Expansion, Rate of Growth and Employment," *Econometrica* 14 (April 1946): 136-47.

5. See A. C. Pigou, *Economics of Welfare* (London: Macmillan, 1932), p. 25.

6. See Mishan, *Technology and Growth.*

7. See Robert Solo, "Technical Change and the Aggregate Production Function," *Review of Economics and Statistics* 39 (August 1957): 312-20; Olavi Niitamo, "Development of Productivity in Finnish Industry, 1925-1952," *Productivity Measurement Review* no. 16 (February 1959): 35-50.

8. For an excellent but intricate summary and critique of this literature, see Mary Jean Bowman, "Education and Economic Growth," *Economic Factors Affecting the Financing of Education,* eds. Roe L. Johns et al. (Gainesville, Fla.: National Educational Finance Project, 1970), esp. pp. 85-86.

9. Fritz Machlup, *Education and Economic Growth* (Lincoln, Nebr.: University of Nebraska Press, 1970), pp. 7-8.

10. Edward F. Denison, *Why Growth Rates Differ* (Washington, D.C.: Brookings, 1967), p. 202.

11. For a brief and lucid account of the methodology of such studies, see Machlup, *Education and Economic Growth,* pp. 10-15.

12. See Robert M. Solow, *Capital Theory and the Rate of Return* (Amsterdam: North-Holland, 1963).

13. Theodore W. Schultz, "Education and Economic Growth," *Social Forces Influencing American Education,* ed. Nelson B. Henry (Chicago: University of Chicago Press, 1961), pp. 46-88.

14. T. W. Schultz, "Rise in the Capital Stock Represented by

Education in the U. S., 1900-1957," *Economics of Higher Education,* ed. Selma J. Mushkin (Washington, D.C.: U. S. Department of HEW, Office of Education, 1962), pp. 93-101.

15. See Theodore W. Schultz, "The Human Capital Approach to Education," *Economic Factors Affecting the Financing of Education,* p. 34.

16. M. J. Bowman, "Human Capital: Concepts and Measure ," *Economics of Higher Education.*

17. Machlup, *Education and Economic Growth,* pp. 13-15.

18. For detailed criticism of Denison's methodology and calculations, see *The Residual Factor and Economic Growth,* which unintentionally was a symposium of his work.

19. Bowman, "Education and Economic Growth," pp. 96-100.

20. Ibid., pp. 110-111. Also, see R. R. Nelson and E.S.Phelps, "Investment in Humans, Technological Diffusion and Economic Growth," *American Economic Review* 56 (May 1956): 69-76.

Chapter 6
Education and International Trade

1. For example, see Edward Denison, *Why Growth Rates Differ* (Washington, D.C.: Brookings Institution, 1967), and Anne Krueger, "Factor Endowments and per Capita Income Differences among Countries," *Economic Journal* (September 1968): 641-59.

2. See *Economic Report of the President 1972* (Washington, D.C.: Government Printing Office, 1972); and *The Manpower Report of the President* (Washington, D.C.: Government Printing Office, 1972).

3. E. Heckscher, "The Effect of Foreign Trade on the Distribution of Income," in A.S. Ellis and L.A. Metzler, eds., *Readings in the Theory of International Trade* (Homewood, Ill.: Irwin, 1950), pp. 272-301; B. Ohlin, *Interregional and International Trade* (Cambridge, Mass.: Harvard University Press, 1933); Paul Samuelson, "International Factor-Price Equalization Once Again," *Economic Journal* 59 (June 1949): 181-97.

4. P. Kenen, "Nature, Capital and Trade," *Journal of Political Economy* 73 (October 1965): 437-60.

5. D. Keesing, "Labor Skills and the Structure of Trade in

Manufactures," in P. Kenen and R. Lawrence, eds., *The Open Economy: Essays on International Trade and Finance* (New York: Columbia University Press, 1968), pp. 3-18.

6. Ibid., p. 11.

7. R. Baldwin, "Determinants of the Commodity Structure of U. S. Trade," *American Economic Review* 61 (March 1971): 126-46. Also see P. Kenen, "Skills, Human Capital, and Comparative Advantage," in *Education, Income and Human Capital,* W. Hansen, ed. (New York: Columbia University Press, 1970), pp. 195-229 and W. Branson, "U. S. Comparative Advantage: Some Further Results," *Brookings Papers on Economic Activity* 3 (1971): 754-59, for further empirical support.

8. Baldwin, "Determinants of the Commodity Structure," pp. 134-36.

9. The following section draws from J. Morrall, *Human Capital, Technology, and the U. S. Role in International Trade* (Gainesville, Fla.: University of Florida Press, 1972), Ch. 3.

10. Baldwin, "Determinants of the Commodity Structures," p. 134.

11. J. Mincer, "On-the-job Training: Costs, Returns, and Some Implications," *Journal of Political Economy* 70 (October 1962): 73.

12. The new attack on the relevance of human capital theory ranges from I. Berg, *Education and Jobs: The Great Training Robbery* (New York: Praeger, 1970); and H. Gintis, "Education, Technology, and the Characteristics of Worker Productivity," *American Economic Review* 61 (May 1971): 266-79; to L. Thurow, "Education and Economic Equality," *Public Interest* 28 (Summer 1972): 66-81.

13. See M. Posner, "International Trade and Technical Change," *Oxford Economic Papers* (October 1961): 321-41; and R. Vernon, "International Investment and International Trade in the Product Cycle," *Quarterly Journal of Economics* 80 (May 1966): 190-207.

14. See D. Keesing, "The Impact of Research and Development on United States Trade," in the *Open Economy,* pp. 175-89; W. Gruber, D. Mehta, and R. Vernon, "The R & D Factor in International Trade and International Investment of United States Industries," *Journal of Political Economy* 75 (February 1967): 20-37; and

..v. Gruber and R. Vernon, "The Technology Factor in a World Trade Matrix," in R. Vernon, ed., *The Technology Factor in International Trade* (New York: Columbia University Press, 1970), pp. 233-72.

15. See the articles by Baldwin, Keesing, "The Impact of Research and Development," and Gruber, Mehta, and Vernon.

16. See Baldwin, "Determinants of the Commodity Structure," and Morrall, *Human Capital.*

17. Baldwin, Kenen, and Hufbauer, "The Impact of National Characteristics and Technology on the Commodity Composition of Trade in Manufactured Goods," in *The Technology Factor in International Trade,* pp. 145-232, have all come to this conclusion.

18. See J. Bhagwati, "The Pure Theory of International Trade: A Survey," *Economic Journal* 74 (March 1964) for this distinction.

19. See Morrall, *Human Capital,* Ch. 4.

20. G. Psacharapoulos and K. Hinchliffe, "Further Evidence of Substitution among Different Types of Educated Labor," *Journal of Political Economy* 80 (July 1972), pp. 786-92.

21. Psacharapoulos and Hinchliffe, "Further Evidence," present empirical support for this proposition.

22. See M. Bowman, "Education and Economic Growth," in this volume; and R. Nelson and E. Phelps, "Investment in Humans and Technological Diffusion and Economic Growth," *American Economic Review* 56 (May 1966): 59-75.

23. F. Welch, "Education in Production," *Journal of Political Economy* 78 (January 1970): 35-59.

24. See H. Leibenstein, "Allocative Efficiency vs. X-Efficiency," *American Economic Review* 56 (June 1966): 392-415.

25. Krueger, "Factor Endowments," p. 658.

26. Bowman, "Education and Economic Growth," also makes this point.

27. See Kenen, "Skills, Human Capital, and Comparative Advantage," p. 209; and Keesing, "Labor Skills and the Structure of Trade in Manufacturing," p. 6.

28. See B. Weisbrod, "Education and Investment in Human Capital," *Journal of Political Economy* 70 (October 1962): 118-19.

29. *Economic Report of the President: 1971* (Washington: Government Printing Office, 1971), p. 99.

30. Calculated by Thurow, "Education and Economic Equality," p. 75.

31. Calculated from Edwin Mansfield, *The Economics of Technological Change* (New York: Norton, 1968), p. 163.

32. *Economic Report of the President, 1972,* p. 130.

33. Calculated from the *Budget of the United States Government: FY 1972* (Washington, D.C.: Government Printing Office, 1972), p. 131.

... deadline for January 31 ... or ... submitted ...

... Scheduled and Dber, amended ... ... Dec ...
... ...
... ... Statistics of the Premium ... ...
... lation from the Bureau ... the United States ...
... ... 1972, Washington, D.C., Government Printing Office,
... p. 123.

Index

111

About the Authors

J. Ronnie Davis was graduated from the University of Southern Mississippi in 1963 and received the Ph.D. in economics from the University of Virginia in 1967. He won the Tipton R. Snavely Prize for the best dissertation completed during 1966/67. From 1967 through 1971, he held the ranks of assistant and associate professor of economics at Iowa State University (Ames). In 1971, he joined the faculty at the University of Florida, where he is professor of economics. Dr. Davis is the author of several monographs and books, including *The New Economics and the Old Economists* (Iowa State University Press, 1971). He has published widely in scholarly journals in economics and political science, and serves on the editorial board of *Public Finance Quarterly*.

John F. Morrall III graduated from Tufts University in 1965 and received the Ph.D. in economics from the University of North Carolina (Chapel Hill) in 1971. From 1969 to 1974, he was an assistant professor of economics at the University of Florida. He has also worked as a social science research analyst for the U.S. Department of Labor and the Housing and Urban Development as a Brookings Institution Economic Policy Fellow. In that capacity he was responsible for evaluating educational, occupational health and safety, equal opportunity, and subsidized housing programs. Dr. Morrall is the author of *Human Capital, Technology, and the U.S. Role in International Trade* (University of Florida Press), as well as articles on economics which have appeared in scholarly journals.